D0396269

12 STEPS TO
SELF-PARENTING
For Adult Children Of Alcoholics

Philip Oliver-Diaz
Patricia A. O'Gorman

Health Communications, Inc.
Deerfield Beach, Florida

Philip Oliver-Diaz, M.S.W.
Patricia A. O'Gorman, Ph.D.
O'Gorman Diaz Inc.
East Chatham, New York

Library of Congress Cataloging-in-Publication Data

Oliver-Diaz, Philip, 1948-
    12 steps to self-parenting for adult children of alcoholics / by
Philip Oliver-Diaz and Patricia A. O'Gorman.
        p.   cm.
        ISBN 0-932194-68-0
        1. Adult children of alcoholics. 2. Self. I. O'Gorman, Patricia
    A. II. Title. III. Title: Twelve steps to self-parenting for adult
children of alcoholics.
HV5132.054 1988   88-7192
362.2'92-- dc19   CIP

© 1988 Patricia A. O'Gorman and Philip Oliver-Diaz

ISBN 0-932194-68-0

Published by: Health Communications, Inc.
                Enterprise Center
                3201 S.W. 15th Street
                Deerfield Beach, FL 33442

Acknowledgments

For each of us there are people whose support and help have made all the difference.

To Peter, Gary, and Marie for their continued support.

To our families, both biological and adopted, our friends, like Jody McPhillips and Dayashakti, and our special loved ones, Sharon, Rob, Jeremy and Michael, for their love and support.

Dedication from Pat: To Michael and Jeremy, my sons and greatest teachers, may you always keep the way clear to your inner child and Higher Parent.

Dedication from Phil: To Trina Diaz Whitener, Mike Diaz, Sr., and Charles Whitener in the spirit of forgiveness and to my nephew, Mike Diaz, Jr., who is an example of courage for us all.

To Our Friends
Who Read This Book

Are you interested in learning more about parenting, self-parenting and inner child work?

Drop us a note if you would like to attend:

— **a SELF-PARENTING Retreat or Seminar**
— **a BREAKING THE CYCLE Parenting Seminar or Workshop**

Please also let us know if you would like to have more information on:

— **INNER CHILD audio tapes and educational material**
— **PARENTING audio and video tapes and educational material**

Write to O'Gorman and Diaz, Inc., 568 Columbia Turnpike, East Greenbush, NY 12061 or call (518) 477-4625.

Love,
Pat and Phil

Introduction

Freeing Your Inner Child —
The Path To Recovery

Your Higher Parent And Your Inner Child

Each of us is composed of two vital selves, an inner child and a Higher Parent. Your inner child is the center of your love, your feelings, your spontaneity, your curiosity. It is the part of you which is exquisitely alive, vital, creative and from which you draw your energy. It is the part of yourself that feels your pain that needs love and support and feels hopeless without it.

Your Higher Parent is the center of your inner wisdom, your intuitive knowledge. This is your problem-solving self, the part of you that will in healthy families gently and lovingly guide your inner child. This is also the part of you who protects your inner child. Your Higher Parent is the part of you unaffected by your ego or your feelings. It is the transcendent part of yourself, a direct channel to your Higher Power.

Vulnerable Cores

The vulnerable cores of your being can become traumatized by living in an actively or passively abusive alcoholic family or a similarly dysfunctional family. And when traumatized, your inner child, deprived of the wisdom of your Higher Parent, may develop defenses that result in what we call a compulsive dependent, and others call a co-dependent, orientation to the world.

The Compulsive Dependent Self

With compulsive dependency, the inner child is locked away for fear that her spontaneity will cause embarrassment, humiliation or worse, overwhelming pain. The voice of the Higher Parent is silenced for fear that it will rock the family's precarious boat, resulting in rejection.

The compulsively dependent self that emerges is often controlling and needing to rescue others, or in turn to be rescued by them. Or due to their compulsive dependency, they will turn to other things in their search for complete-ness, such as compulsively overeating, compulsive sex, compulsively spending money or working excessively, all in an attempt to be filled up.

Compulsive dependent individuals learn to exist as a half-person, only complete when something or someone external to them can be drawn into them. They have lost access to their inner child. And as a result they have lost their capacity for playfulness, intimacy and true sexuality. They have lost access to their Higher Parent, and deprived of inner guidance, they repeat these unsuccessful patterns in each new relationship that they form.

The Promises Of Self-Parenting

Self-parenting is about freeing your inner child and releasing the voice of your Higher Parent, about accepting and nurturing yourself. The promise of self-parenting is that you will be able to live in the present and leave the past behind and learn to unconditionally love yourself. Based on the Twelve Steps of Alcoholics Anonymous, the *12 Steps To Self-Parenting* is about granting yourself a second chance to parent the child within. It is about learning to nurture yourself through self-forgiveness.

It is about letting God into your life and learning to reach out for love. It is about letting go of the baggage of the past and healing old wounds, and learning how not to recreate these painful patterns in your present. It is about allowing your inner child to be spontaneous, joyful, alive, free. It is about allowing your Higher Parent to guide you with your inner wisdom.

It is about learning to join your Higher Parent and inner child in a healthy manner, making true intimacy with others possible, allowing you to break the bonds of isolation and compulsive or co-dependent behavior. It is about learning through healthy self-parenting to use our Higher Parent as a beacon of light to guide us through the storms and dark times, while your inner child releases the healing energy of love and makes it available to you and those around you.

All of these constitute the total process of recovery. Self-parenting is about the long road home — the road from loneliness and self-doubt, to self-validation, unconditional self-love and intimacy. The road from the pain of the past to the joy, unconditional self love and fullness of the present.

Contents

Surrendering: To Our Love For Our Inner Child

A.A. Step 1: We admitted that we were powerless over alcohol — that our lives had become unmanageable.

Self-Parenting Step 1: Admitted our powerlessness to change our past — that our lives had become unmanageable and became willing to surrender to our love and not to our fear.

The Struggle To Control

The Greeks had a wonderful story in their mythology about Sisyphus, who would take a rock up a hill, and having got to the top of the hill, the rock would roll down again. This was shown to be an exercise in futility, and also show us that although humans may seek to arrange the affairs of their lives, those things having once been arranged have a nasty habit of rearranging themselves to suit themselves.

Now a rock is a thing more apt to stay in place than human consciousness. And imagine if a rock rolls back down a hill, what it is like to try to manipulate human brains. So Sisyphus had only the frustration of the rock, while others have had the frustration of trying to push others' minds up the hill, only to have them roll down before they got to the top.

*The words of Prahsingh in **Brother Lion**, 1987*

Control's Seduction

Like Sisyphus, each of us tries to control. But unlike Sisyphus, the goal of our control is something often larger and more complicated than a rock. More often when we try to control ourselves, we close down our feelings. Or we try to control others. We tell them what to feel, how to feel and more importantly what to do. And we try to control our environment. We spend an enormous amount of emotional energy visualizing our husband home from work first as we drive up to the house with a car full of groceries, just as perhaps we tried as a child to visualize our father not drinking as we came home from school.

If we have come from a home with alcoholism, gambling, the mental illness of a parent or sibling, or any other sustained trauma, our need to control is a survival tactic, a way that our inner child sought to protect us from what felt at times to be a hostile world.

We learned to believe that we had control, perhaps even supernatural control. To acknowledge that neither we nor even our parents were in charge would have felt overwhelming, and left us feeling alone and abandoned. And because occasionally some of what we tried to control occurred, we would come home from school praying for a sober father, and if we found him so, we began to believe that we had power.

So we learned to try to control everything around us. The promise that we made ourselves, was that if we controlled the outcome, the outcome would not be negative. Unknowingly our inner child signed on to blame himself for all the negative outcomes that were just beyond his control. And when we failed at controlling ourselves or events around us, we took it as a personal failure.

For many of us who grew up in an alcoholic or other addicted or traumatic home, our drug is control. Like any other drug, control is addicting. Recovery for us now begins by our addressing this drug, control.

Our Guide: Our Higher Parent

The impossibility of control as simply illustrated by *Brother Lion,* makes it clear that we have no real control, except within ourselves. And within each of us we have our Higher Parent to guide us, so that our inner child does not need to be troubled with the child's solution to feeling overwhelmed, which is our child's need to control. Following the counsel of our Higher Parent is our way out of being a "control junkie".

The Price Our Inner Child Pays For Our Need To Control

Unmanageability In Our Lives

When we try to control what cannot be controlled, we doom ourselves to feel that life is unmanageable. And if our goal, control, is where we put all of our energy, if here is where we choose to put our great resources of creativity, our spiritual energy, our love, then we will be constantly frustrated as was Sisyphus. Our lives will feel unmanageable, for they *will be* unmanageable.

Lack Of Intimacy: Compulsive Self-Reliance

In the attempt to control everyone and everything around us we become obsessed with being totally self-reliant. We believe in our drive to control that our self-will can make anything we want to happen. We close out people, refuse help and deny our need for the support and the comfort for which our inner child cries. We learn to live in a desert, we learn to live in isolation, we create a world in which we are all we need to get by. We become compulsive about being self-reliant to such a degree that when we finally need to let others help us, we can't or don't know how. And so husbands, wives, lovers and friends leave us because they feel useless and unnecessary. And we remain alone in our totally controlled self-imposed prison, in solitary confinement and we forget that we have the key to set ourselves free, our Higher Parent.

Lack Of Spontaneity

When we become a "control junkie", we trade away a very important part of our inner child. We give up our spontaneity. We came to believe that if we could master controlling ourselves, then we could control others. And what do we master? We master our spontaneity — that part of us where our inner child is at free play, where our inner child delights in what is in the world around him. We squelch our spontaneity for we feel that the world is too dangerous. We protect our inner child, by locking it up, and we rejoice that we have the power to do so.

Feelings Of Guilt

Since we feel that we can control the world around us, we become responsible for this world. We take on responsibility for the actions of others. Since in our control we are not doing a very good job, for things keep happening differently than what we hoped and prayed for, we feel guilty.

Lack Of Love

As we try to control our life we begin to unconsciously pare down what we allow into our life. We become overwhelmed with the magnitude of what we are attempting to influence, and to protect ourselves we begin to reduce our vista and lessen what we will allow in. When we do this, we also reduce our access to the good feelings that surround us. We minimize or even dispel the love that exists in the world for us. As a result we feel empty for we are full of the illusion or delusion of control in the place where there could have been love.

Inability To Resolve And Forgive Childhood Traumas

When we try to control, we emotionally freeze ourselves for we cannot easily control just one part of ourselves. As a result we tend to try to control everything. And like a bad dream that we cannot shake, our childhood traumas still haunt us. We retraumatize ourselves by their constant memory. And since we are trying to control our memories, as opposed to accepting them, they stay in our consciousness.

And As A Result The Inability To Move On With Our Life

If only we could allow our past, accept it and not put all of our energy into controlling it. Imagine how handicapped we would be if we were conscious all day long of our right hand. It would dominate our life. When we give any part of ourselves this much attention, then we keep it in our mind. This is why our past can be so much a part of our present. We need to learn to give the painful memories of our childhood only special attention when they require it. Then we would be able to resolve these painful memories.

A Season For Grieving — And Forgiveness

This does not mean we should deny the pain of the past nor that we should not work through this pain. It means that for everything there is a season. There is a time to grieve in the winter of our pain and a time to understand the how and why of our pain in the season of integration, the spring of our recovery. There is a season of resolution in our blossoming summer when we accept what has happened, and finally there is a season of harvest when we joyfully forgive the past.

This journey through the seasons is a journey within. A journey in which we are led and supported by our intuitive wisdom, our Higher Parent. The first step of this journey is the admission of the love we have for our inner child and our powerlessness to change the past.

Acknowledging The Unconditional Love We Have For Our Inner Child

Many of us have difficulty in knowing when we are "in love". As a result we have even greater difficulty in knowing if we love ourselves. The work of the Twelve Steps is really a process in determining who we are so that we may truly and unconditionally love our inner child.

Our love for ourselves is first of all based on acceptance, not on self-judgment. To accept ourselves means to know ourselves. No more hiding or pretending, only self-knowledge and acceptance.

Second, our love for ourselves is based on allowing ourselves "to be", "to experience". This means allowing our spontaneity, our curiosity and allowing our "being" without the compulsion "to do". To be is to love. In the words of Prahsingh, "Love is to be, as death is not to be." To love our inner child is to allow, to experience and to be with our inner child.

Surrendering To Our Love

Turning It Over

We need to acknowledge that "we can't". This is a profound statement. In this statement we relinquish the control that in reality we do not really possess over our life. In relinquishing control, we hand over our need for control and order in our life to our intuitively knowing supportive self — our Higher Parent — and to our God. We need to turn our life over to our Higher Power to lead us, lest we bloody ourselves by batting our head against the wall of control.

But, as Prahsingh says,"In the long run the Creator will have Its way, you might as well (go with it), rather than against it." For us this means we learn to turn over our need for control.

Allowing Inner Peace

Our power lies in how we define our life. We can define ourselves as someone who cannot make it happen, as someone who tries hard but "luck" is against us — yes, we can choose to be a victim!

Or we see ourselves in harmony within ourselves and within the universe. We can see that whatever happens to us is our destiny, which we accept and learn from. When we learn from our life, and accept our past, present and our future, we can have the type of inner peace that allows our child within to rest in the assurance that explorations into the world will be safe.

Acknowledging Our Fear

With our love and commitment to our inner child comes fear for the well-being of our inner child. As a way of trying to control our fear, we try to control our love. As a result we begin to smother what we love the most, our inner child.

We need to learn to acknowledge our fear and as the Bene Gesserit say in **DUNE**, we need to: Watch fear come towards us. Allow fear to enter us. And watch the path that fear makes as it leaves us. Allowing ourselves to feel fear is a self-loving act, for our feelings are a vital part of our inner child.

So We May Acknowledge Our Love

Acknowledging our love means being vulnerable. And as we know, being vulnerable is the opposite of control. To allow our love means to open our heart, to open our feelings, to be guided by the knowledge of our Higher Parent and the freedom of our inner child, free, unprotected, rejoicing. Yes, we can be shot down. Our love doesn't protect us. But our love can guide us as no other emotion can. Our love can allow us to soar with the birds, to swim within the waters of the earth. Our love can bring us to places where we did not know we could exist, places of peace and strength. Our love brings us riches that no other emotion can hold.

Meditations On Parenting Your Inner Child

Surrender to your love for your inner child. Bask in this love. Know that you cannot love yourself too much. Your love may have no end. To own your love is to be able to be guided by allowing yourself to witness your love's effect upon you.

Share your love. Allow yourself to be vulnerable to your love of yourself and your love of others. And in this sharing of your love, know that you will have the gift of intimacy.

Allow the knowledge of your Higher Parent to be deep within yourself. Know that to own this knowledge is not to be ruled by it, but to be guided by the wisest part of who you truly are.

Daily Self-Parenting Affirmations

I will surrender to my love, knowing that the strength I derive from this makes me more power-ful.

I will be guided by my love and not my need to control, knowing that my control is bred only by fear, but my love is derived from God.

I will acknowledge my fear, and love myself through this feeling, seeking only to learn what it has to teach me.

Overcoming Abandonment

A.A. Step 2: Came to believe that a Power greater than ourselves could restore us to sanity.

Self-Parenting Step 2: Found hope in the belief that recovery is possible through faith and an acceptance of the fact that we are never really alone.

Footprints

One night an old man had a dream that he had died and gone to heaven, where he was given a chance to review the footsteps of his life. He looked down and noticed that all over the dark valleys and difficult places he had traveled, there was only one set of footprints, but over the plains and across the beautiful mountains there were two sets of footprints as if someone had walked by his side.

He turned to the Lord and said, "There is something I can't understand about my life on earth. Why is it that across the mountains and over the smooth plains and easy places you have walked by my side, but here over the rough and difficult places I have walked alone, for I see in these places there is just one set of footprints?"

The Lord turned to the man and said, "It is true that while your life was easy I walked along by your side. I was Your companion, but here when the walking was hard, and the path was difficult, here where you crossed the battlefields of life and did not have the strength to endure, I realized that that was the time you needed me most.

"And that is why I carried you."

Anonymous

Emotional Abandonment

Like the man in the story many of us have felt abandoned by our Higher Power. It is hard for adult children of alcoholics and other people brought up in traumatic families to imagine that they were protected during the difficult times in their childhood. Those of us having grown up in such homes are used to seeing only one set of footprints.

Having grown up in families driven by crisis and self-centeredness we learned to accept that we were not going to be attended to by our parents in the way we wanted or needed to be. Some of us were able to establish a strong connection to our Higher Power during childhood as a way of feeling less abandoned. But most of us suffered a loss of faith as we realized that our parents had seemingly abdicated their responsibility to nurture and protect us.

Love Was Present But Unavailable

Some of us grew up in homes where death or divorce actually separated us from one or both of our parents. For others of us, because of the crisis in our homes, we were shuttled off to relatives, friends or foster homes. But most of us grew up in homes with our parents.

We often forget that our parents are probably themselves adult children of alcoholics. They, too, have suffered as children. They did not have the benefit of a movement for adult children like we do to help them heal. They were forced to parent us in the dark. All they had to go by was the way they were parented.

We tend to forget how little was known about alcoholism and child abuse even 20 years ago, much less 30 or 40 years ago. Our parents did the only thing they could, they carried on the tradition of self-centered or abusive parenting that they were brought up with. If they were struck as children, they struck us. If they were humiliated, they humiliated us. Not out of spite or hate but out of loyalty to their parents.

Our parents tried their best by following the traditions of previous generations. Unfortunately these were traditions of self-centered parenting, traditions of child-rearing through crisis and sometimes traditions of child-rearing through physical violence. This left us the legacy of living with chaos, abuse and learned helplessness. It was not the legacy they intended for us, they wanted the best for us, they just did not know how to go about it.

They loved us but did not know how to show their love. Love was present in them but unavailable to us. We did not understand this as children. Many of our parents were never taught how to show love, so they could not show it to us, much less each other. And we drew the conclusion that as we were not loved, we were unlovable. We were wrong.

Children Of Loyalty

Many of our parents may have gone through even more traumatic childhoods than we did. Most of us didn't learn the truth about our parents' childhoods until we were adults. Many of us still don't know what our parents' childhoods were like. Often our parents made up stories about their childhood to protect us from the truth about our grandparents, thinking they were saving us from trauma. They took an unspoken vow of silence concerning their parents and their lives as children, leaving us in the dark and feeling resentful. They loved their parents and stayed loyal to their parents by continuing dysfunctional traditions of parenting and interacting.

We stayed loyal and protective of our parents, even when they hurt us, the same way they stayed loyal to their parents. We took care to make sure that no one found out how we really lived. Sometimes we invented fantasy parents to replace the ones we had. All to protect them, just as they had protected their parents and so we continue a family tradition of secrecy out of loyalty.

Or we sacrificed ourselves. We made ourselves responsible for all the family problems as a way of hiding from the truth that our parents were not all that we needed. Or we tried to deal with the family's problems alone, which in some cases left us being physically abused or sexually molested. And yet we kept the secret. Whether our parents were alcoholic, compulsive gamblers, compulsive eaters, workaholics or addicted to each other the result was the same. We grew up feeling emotionally abandoned by our parents.

We waited and hoped and waited and hoped for when we would be taken care of, but in the end after much disappointment, our hope was replaced with bitterness. We shut down our hearts and pretended we no longer cared whether we were taken care of or not. We may have even convinced ourselves that we were nurtured as young children, but our heart told us otherwise. It was a way of maintaining our loyalty to our family, a way of loving our family, a way of holding back our pain. So many of us ignored this seemingly emotional abandonment by our parents, and pretended it never happened, while a subtle wall of bitterness encased our heart.

Abandonment By God

This emotional abandonment by our parents laid the groundwork for all our future relationships including our relationship with God. For some of us these feelings of abandonment extend to feeling abandoned by God for leaving us in such difficult conditions. Like the man in the story, we only see one set of footprints and we falsely believe those footprints are our own. In this false belief we make our self-reliance into a God. We worship our invulnerability and we become compulsively self-reliant. We are thankful that we do not allow anyone close enough to touch us, let alone harm us, and we feel that this is success. But within our heart, we feel bereft of hope. Our aloneness is translated into a belief that we were abandoned by God and so we lost our faith.

This attitude towards God creates a legacy of hopelessness and fear. Instead of living in a world where on its most basic level we are loved and cared for, we create worlds of mistrust and fear. We create a world in which we only believe in ourselves. As a result we feel borderline rage, helplessness and utter aloneness.

Compulsive Self-Reliance . . . When We Become God

In the end we become God as a defense against feeling how needy and scared we really are. We create a world where only the fittest survive. We create a world devoid of compassion and fellowship. We create a world in which dependence on self is everything.

This dependence on self replaces dependence on God and interdependence with others. It creates a false sense of power, a feeling of omnipotence based on utter self-control.

As we learned in Step One, in order to accomplish this self-control we limit our lives to a small area, one where only our most basic needs are met. Compassion, love and sharing become impossible.

After a while this self-control and self-reliance becomes a compulsive behavior, one we can no longer stop. Like an alcoholic, we are no longer able to stop without help. We have become compulsively self-reliant, unable to let anyone in, our personal relationships having been sacrificed.

Ultimately, as we replace God with our addiction to relying on ourselves, we become completely isolated from others. In the end we create continual abandonment scenarios as friends, lovers, husbands and wives leave us because they feel unneeded by us, because they feel unwanted by us and because we have such a reliance on our own self, they feel there is no room in our lives for them.

Finally we are left all alone caught in a cage of our own making — prisoners of our own competence and resourcefulness. We have become God ruling over a very small world with one inhabitant.

Abandonment By Others . . . Being Addicted To Empty Wells

Just as we can become addicted to being self-reliant as an outcome of feeling abandoned by God, we can also become addicted to being abandoned by others. Many of us have learned to survive with minimal expectations from life. We have learned not to expect much from our parents, from our mates or from our co-workers. We look for relationships with people who are not able to meet our emotional needs. We become addicted to people who are empty wells, people who will not be there for us because of their own personal limitations.

In this way we maintain our ties to our childhood by choosing people to marry, to live with and to love, who have the same limitations we have experienced in our family. In some ways this may seem nurturing to us. Being disappointed is something we are used to at least. In this way we continue to re-enact scenes from our childhood, we continue a tradition of being abandoned by others. Out of bitterness and confusion we continue to create scenarios of abandonment in our lives.

Full Wells — The Path To Fulfillment

Most of us simply do not know what it feels like to have our needs meet. We accept what we have because we are not aware of the alternative. Being abandoned by God and others seems to be our inevitable fate. We do not recognize that people who are full wells, people who are capable of giving love and support, people who would stand by us really do exist.

We do not believe that abundance and fulfillment are our true legacy. We may even feel that love is dangerous. With no belief in a Higher Power, with no faith that recovery is possible, feeling utterly alone, we are stuck in our own mistrust.

In order to break this cycle of abandonment and despair we need to challenge these basic assumptions about life. We need to allow ourselves to feel protected and loved by the good people around us who we so often reject. We need to allow ourselves to have faith again in the good things that life has to offer. We need to find the courage to allow ourselves to experience full wells, trusting that God will give us what we need in order to let go of our fear of fulfillment.

The Way Back To God — Our Highest Parent

The way back to God is to allow your Higher Parent to guide your inner child to create a new family tradition of fulfillment. We need to understand that our Higher Parent has always been available to us to guide and protect us. We need to accept that in the end it is not our parents or God who have abandoned us, we have abandoned ourselves.

When we divest ourselves of the love from our inner child and the wisdom of our Higher Parent we truly abandon the best within ourselves. Our Higher Parent is the discriminating part of ourselves that will shape a new life of positive choices if we follow its guidance. Our Higher Parent can teach us how to surround ourselves with people who are full wells.

If we allow ourselves to be carried by our Higher Parent and by God and surrender to the belief that recovery is possible, we can find our way back to our true home, our spiritual home. If we allow ourself to rekindle our faith in God and ask for guidance from our Higher Parent, we will never be alone again.

When we allow our Higher Parent to teach our inner child how to break the cycle of compulsive self-reliance and empty well relationships, we acknowledge we are not alone. We become strong in the belief that it is possible to change and recover from the trauma of our childhood.

Replacing Fear With Faith

Faith is the act of trusting in the guidance of your Higher Parent. Yes, this will feel extreme. Yes, it will involve a major risk. But one of the strengths that many adult children of alcoholics have is the ability to risk. This ability to go for broke and risk may as well work for you as it has so often worked against you.

For adult children trust in anything or anybody is a tall order. It doesn't come easily. Replacing fear with faith needs to be consciously practiced. It is work. We need to be willing to do the necessary self-work to let a Higher Power work in our lives. We need to open the door to allow our Higher Parent to walk through. Having hope and allowing this hope to lead the way for you is new thinking for many ACoAs.

Fear Is A Darkroom Where Negatives Are Developed

All too often fear rules our lives, directing us to stay with what we know, instead of venturing into new territory. We are frightened of change, we fear having our needs met. We see the chance of happiness as a threat to our self-control, and more importantly, as a threat to how we express our love for our family. We unconsciously worry whether we could remain a part of this family if we allow ourself to love and be loved. We fear the bittersweet pain that accompanies feeling loved and the painful memories of childhood that it brings. We need to realize that replacing fear with faith is the beginning of letting go of the past and finding our real recovery from the traumas of our childhood.

Our Inner Child's Spiritual Nature

Unconditional love, trust, intuition, spontaneity and self-affirmation are the true components of our inner child. When we work Step Two, we release the force within us to heal our lives. We do this when we come to believe in a Higher Power and allow this power to manifest within us in the form of our Higher Parent.

We can do this only when we replace fear with faith. Only then do we allow the true nature of our inner child to shine through, and claim our true legacy of abundance and fulfillment and love.

When we let go of self-will and allow a belief in a power greater than ourselves, we claim our true greatness, the real source of all security, the force within us. We allow a greater consciousness to work in our lives, a Higher Parent who will never abandon us.

The Power Within

Each of us is an expression of the divine force. Some people call this divine force God, some call it Allah or the Great Spirit, others simply call it the Force. Whatever you call this power present in our lives, it is the essence of all living things.

For each of us who has been through the long and lonely nights of isolation and fear, who has traveled the difficult places, walked the mountains, for each of us who has overcome addictions to substances and people, the presence of the divinity within, the Higher Parent in each of us is what has sustained us.

In consciously putting faith in that force, in allowing a Higher Power to work in our life, to create health and abundance, we change our family tradition from one of empty promises, empty wells and dashed hopes, to one of fulfillment and creative growth.

The power within is ever present. We may not always feel the presence but when we trust in the knowlege of this existence, we recognize that the divine presence within us will not abandon us. We come to understand that we have and always have had an inner home, full of nurturing and security; we only needed to believe in it for it to be available. In practicing the second step, we release the healing energy of the divine to make miracles of recovery available for all of us.

Meditations On Parenting Your Inner Child

Let yourself know that with faith all things are possible. Remember that fear is a darkroom where negatives are developed. Allow yourself to risk feeling the power of the divinity within you. Simply by acknowledging a Higher Power you release a healing energy into your life.

Recognize that you have always been carried by a power greater than yourself. We all have an inner home and a Higher Parent who will never abandon us. While we may have been abandoned on an emotional level by our parents, on a spiritual level we have always been nurtured and loved.

Claim the true nature of your inner child. The child within is essentially unconditional love. The child within is full of trust, intuition, spontaneity and self-affirmation. When we claim the true nature of our inner child, we affirm our real legacy of love. Allow yourself to visualize a world where you are loved and love others.

Daily Self-Parenting Affirmations

I acknowledge that I can never really be abandoned, that I have an inner home and a greater source of nurturing, my Higher Power and my Higher Parent.

I affirm my right to be loved and supported and to share my life with full wells.

I believe in a greater good expressed in a loving God, who is ever present to guide me through my recovery.

I replace fear with faith and turn my personal darkness into light.

I affirm the spiritual nature of my inner child, which is all-embracing unconditional love. I create a vision of myself in recovery full of lightness, forgiveness and self-validation.

CHAPTER 3

Struggling To Trust:
Hard Pain — Soft Pain

A.A. Step 3: *Made a decision to turn our will and our lives over to the care of God as we understood Him.*

Self-Parenting Step 3: Learn to let go of compulsive self-reliance by reaching out to our Higher Parent.

The Tiger, The Man And God

A man was being chased by a tiger. He ran as hard as he could until he was at the edge of a cliff with the tiger in hot pursuit. The man looked over the edge of the cliff and saw a branch growing out from the side of the cliff a few feet down. He jumped down and grabbed the branch just as the tiger reached the cliff. The tiger growled viciously as the man sighed a great sigh of relief.

Just then a mouse came out from a crevice and began to chew on the branch. The man looked down to what was a drop of a thousand feet and sure death and looked to the heavens and yelled out, "Dear God, if you are there, please help. I will do anything you ask but please help."

Suddenly a voice came booming down from heaven, "You will do anything I ask?" it questioned.

The man shocked to hear a reply to his plea yelled back,"I will gladly do anything you ask, but please save me."

The voice from heaven then replied, "There is one way to save you but it will take courage and faith."

The branch began to weaken from the mouse and the tiger was still growling a few feet above the man, "Please, Lord, tell me what I must do and I will do it. Your will is my will."

The voice from heaven then said, "All right then, let go of the branch."

The man looked down to a fall of a thousand feet and certain death. He looked up at the hungry tiger a few feet away and he looked at the mouse still chewing on the branch. Then he looked up at the heavens and yelled, "Is there anyone else up there?"

Anonymous

Falling Into The Abyss — Letting Go Of Compulsive Self-Reliance

Like the man in the parable we are all holding on for dear life to our branches, asking for help but unwilling to *let go and let God.* Even though our self-will often gets us in trouble, letting go of self-will and compulsive self-reliance is one of the hardest things for us to do. It goes against everything that we have learned as children.

For ACoAs and other adult children of traumatic families, reaching out to God and letting go of self-will feels like falling into an abyss. For many of us it feels like we are going to die when we attempt to break the pattern of compulsive self-reliance. It is like letting go of the branch in the parable . . . we are terrified that we won't survive.

Compulsive Self-Reliance

We have been taught to be self-sufficient at all costs and to trust only in our will to make things happen. Our trust in our will and the belief that we are alone in the world, leaves us secretly bitter, and hopeless, although the world rarely sees that face. As we learned in Step Two, our belief in our ability to control often replaces any belief we had as a child in a Higher Power.

For our inner child, self-will and total self-reliance is the only way she knows to protect herself. This self-sufficiency, therefore, becomes part of our storehouse of compulsive behavior. Eventually because of our lack of faith in Higher Power we became compulsively self-reliant, not even being able to be given to by our loved ones, who resent us for acting superior. This reliance on self often leads to difficulty in relationships with others and an inability to form intimate relationships.

Compulsive self-reliance is the disease of our self-will. It comes from our belief that we can change the past through our personal efforts if we only try hard enough. Compulsive self-reliance keeps the child within us frightened and hopeless. It keeps our inner child stuck in the pain of our childhood — the hard pain of denial. Only by letting go of our absolute reliance on self-will and reaching out to God can we take the first steps to free the child within. Only by allowing our Higher Parent (the intuitive knowledge within each of us) to guide us can we learn to let go and let God.

Reaching Out To God, To Our Higher Parent And To Each Other

We are taught to keep secrets even from God. We are taught that sharing ourselves and our personal lives with others is bad and dangerous. We learn that being loyal to our family means not reaching out for help. We learn to live alone.

The reality is we cannot live without help. Our self-will and compulsive self-reliance have led us down the path of isolation, fear and loneliness. Our unwillingness to lean on our Higher Power and others for help has left us hopeless and exhausted, and sometimes physically ill. Our inability to reach out and become vulnerable has made it impossible for us to find fulfillment emotionally or sexually. And finally our anger at God has left us floundering in despair for meaning in our lives beyond sheer survival.

The first step to entering the world is to reach out to God and your Higher Parent. This first reaching out will open a door that will allow you to access limitless real security, comfort and inner knowledge. Once we break our family tradition of secrecy and isolation and let God and our Higher Parent in, we become willing to let people come closer as well. We can slowly let go of our compulsive self-reliance and allow ourselves to be guided by a greater consciousness.

God, The Ultimate Parent

How many times have we called God "Our Father"?

Trusting in God creates an inner home that can never be violated. God, as you understand Him, can be a source of comfort and safety that no one can take away. A good parent provides direction and lends support but many of us have grown up without support or direction. Therefore, God can provide, through your Higher Parent, the direction and the support your inner child needs and deserves.

Our Higher Parent is our direct channel to God. When we let go of our self-will and our compulsive self-reliance, we let a greater will emerge through our Higher Parent. Just as the inner child asserts herself in our life, so our Higher Parent's inner wisdom can lead us and is always available.

If we allow it, turning our will over to God will create a real sense of security that comes from no longer needing to be always in control. But allowing your Higher Parent and God to lead the way is full of risks. Like the man holding onto the branch in the story, we may not want to trust what we are told when the road appears too dangerous.

For most of us living with acceptance and love will seem alien and scary. We will resist, like our friend holding onto the branch, letting go and trusting. Our self-reliance will look good when we see the road before us leading to uncharted lands, lands of intimacy and sharing. But if we reach out to our Higher Parent for help, we will find our way and land safely in spite of our fears.

The Long Line Of People To Our Heart

For each of us there is a long line of people to our heart, people we loved and lost or people we never had and feel as missing pieces in our lives. As we grow up and toughen ourselves, we shut down our feelings and we close off our heart. Only when we attempt to reach out for help, do we find that the child within has been locked up and with her our ability to love.

Grief And Mourning — The Beginning

Most of us spend our lives protecting ourselves from the reality of our grief and mourning. We do not believe that we can survive facing all of our losses, so we pretend that they didn't happen or had no effect on us. In order to accomplish this we must ignore the emotional reality of our inner child, who recognizes and feels the losses and pain of childhood. We deny the reality of our childhood, thereby failing to help our inner child mourn the past and move on into the present.

Grief and mourning are necessary parts of recovery. It is only by reviewing our past, feeling its reality and making sense of our childhood experience that we truly free ourselves and our inner child. It is only by learning to trust someone, a friend, therapist or ACoA group member, and reach out that we can become safe enough to move beyond our denial into our grief, which is the true beginning of recovery.

In order to free the child within and open our hearts, we must face the need for us to mourn and to feel the reality of our childhood; and in order to trust and reach out to God, we need to allow our Higher Parent to teach our inner child new rules, to teach our inner child that reaching out is a good thing and that acknowledging our real pain will heal us.

Healing The Pain Of Childhood — Learning To Trust

Hard Pain

There are two kinds of pain, soft pain and hard pain. Hard pain is a grating, hollow pain, an unending, numbing pain. Hard pain is the pain of denial. It is the pain that comes from our compulsive self-reliance. It is not a healing pain.

Hard pain does not bring freedom. Hard pain is the pain of fear. Many of us have a great wound in our hearts, a wound created by the abandonment we experienced as a child. Hard pain is the denial of this wound.

Soft pain is the acceptance of this wound.

Hard pain does not free us. It keeps us stuck in the past. It breeds bitterness and resentment. It keeps us in an angry place with our parents. It creates walls and shuts out forgiveness and compassion. It does not allow for resolution and healing. It keeps old wars raging.

Soft Pain

Soft pain is the pain of mourning and loss. It is a source of healing for our inner child. Soft pain is the pain of acceptance and working through.

Soft pain is the pain our inner child feels when our Higher Parent guides her with compassion through the reality of her childhood. Soft pain is the pain we felt as a child when being misled and disappointed. Soft pain hurts deeply but once it is over, it releases healing energy. Soft pain leads to a state of forgiveness for self and others. It allows us to have our feelings while building a healing bridge between ourselves and others in our heart.

Letting Go Of Hate

Our inner child needs to heal. Tears are the coin of healing. Letting go of our hate and resentment and the hard pain that comes with those feelings; and allowing the soft pain of our mourning to wash over us is part of how we can love our inner child and help her heal. Allowing our Higher Parent to lead us in the direction of God's will creates bridges of love, fellowship and forgiveness for us to cross.

Recovery Is A Spiritual Path

The path to recovery is a spiritual path that takes us through our pain to a place of healing and forgiveness. By applying the third step to yourself as you self-parent into a new and more fulfilling life, you will receive a blessing you never thought possible: the discovery of your inner wisdom, your Higher Parent.

By learning to reach out and ask for help, we can begin to turn the valve of living on again. By learning to let go of compulsive self-reliance, we can reach the fullness of expression meant for us as children of the light.

Meditations On Parenting Your Inner Child

Turn over your will to God. Practice seeing yourself as able to let go and let God. Opening your heart to your Higher Power and turning your life over to the care of God *as you understand Him* will allow you to let go of your compulsive self-reliance and make room for a greater force in your life.

Acknowledge you are not alone. Reaching out for help and acknowledging that you are not alone, brings you into the world and out of your isolation. Asking for help creates a vulnerability which invites people into your life. Admitting that there are other people in the world who could care for you, allows you to create a new family tradition full of nurturing and support.

Visualize yourself in a world of loving people. Be gentle with yourself. Remember you have done the best you could do. The child within you needs your help before she will trust because she is frightened. As you self-parent you will need to reassure your inner child that it is okay for you to let go and to trust in God and reach out to others.

Allow your mourning. There is pain associated with being abandoned. We need that pain. It is the doorway to the rest of our emotional life. It is the way into our love for others, the door to fulfilling relationships. Your inner child needs you to let her know that she can survive this pain. It is the pain of healing. Mourning the losses of childhood will allow the light of God to come through. It will allow you to know a greater peace and a true sense of inner security. The soft pain of mourning will allow you to find yourself.

Daily Self-Parenting Affirmations

I affirm that I can reach out to others and let go of my compulsive self-reliance.

I recognize God, as *I understand Him,* as my Higher Parent.

I turn my will over to God and let Him show me the way to parent myself and heal.

I affirm that the only real security is the security of being connected to a power greater than myself and letting that force for good work in my life.

I see myself bathed in light and I know that I can tolerate feeling the pain of my childhood. I recognize the healing quality of the soft pain of mourning.

CHAPTER 4

Accepting Who We Are: The Struggle With Our Dark Side

A.A. Step 4: Made a searching and fearless moral inventory of ourselves.

Self-Parenting Step 4: Made an honest assessment of our strengths and weaknesses and accepted the impact our childhood has had on us as adults.

The Struggle

There is a story told about Abraham, the King and prophet, that goes like this:

It was in biblical times that a young king from a distant land heard of the wisdom and kindness of King Abraham and asked his court astrologers and seers to come and see a protrait of Abraham he had just obtained and tell him what they could see in Abraham's face so that he could be better prepared for meeting with this famous king.

Expecting to hear of evidence of Abraham's fine qualities, the young king was stunned to hear warnings that the face of Abraham did not show kindness and wisdom and the other great virtues for which Abraham was famous but instead showed cruelty and arrogance and a fierce heart full of vengeance. They warned the young king to give up his idea to make a pilgrimage to meet with Abraham for they feared for his life with such a dangerous and heartless fellow. They persisted, but the young king would not relent in his plan to visit the famous King of Israel.

And so it was that the young king from a distant land made his pilgrimage to see Abraham. Taking but a small entourage with him he took leave of his people with a heavy heart, not entirely sure he would ever return again. Upon reaching Abraham's kingdom he asked for an audience with the great King. And on the third day of his visit Abraham granted his wish and the young king met the old and great King of Israel.

As he walked in the room he saw a face full of peace and kindness unlike any face he had ever seen before. He saw a wise and gentle soul full of strength and above all he saw a spritual man full of holiness. After an hour or so of a wonderful conversation in which the young king learned a great deal about himself and being a leader of men, he gathered the courage to ask the great king a question which had disturbed him greatly.

He said, "Dear friend, I do not mean to offend but please answer a question which has troubled me this whole time we have spent together. In preparation for this trip I sought out and bought a painting of you done in your youth. I asked my seers and astrologers to analyze your face so that I might know you better when we met. What they told me troubled me greatly. They said to beware of you for they saw cruelty and vengefulness and arrogance in your face. Yet now as we speak all I feel for you is love and respect and all I see is wisdom and kindness. Please explain this confusion to me if you can."

Abraham smiled gently and said to the young king, "What your seers and court astrologers saw in my face was true. I have all those qualities that they saw in my portrait."

The young king went to protest but Abraham held up his hand to quiet the young king and went on. "What your court astrologers and seers could not see in that portrait of my youth was my struggle to overcome those defects of character. All of us, my young friend, possess a dark side. It is in the struggle to transform those dark qualities into love that we come to know the best in ourselves and reach true communication with God."

Our Dark Side

Like Abraham, each of us have to struggle with our dark side, the part of us that we wish to hide. Just as we have good qualities that enhance our lives, our light side, we have negative qualities that detract from our lives and the lives of those around us.

Many of us attempt to deny or hide the traits of our dark side for fear of judgment from others and sometimes from ourselves. We pretend to be something we are not, or we deny or try to control our past history in the hope that by denying the facts, we can change them.

Fear

It is our fear that gives strength to our dark side. Fear of admitting our human frailties keeps us in hiding. Fear keeps us in ego battles and feeds the need to attack others as a way of protecting ourselves. Fear says that we are strong if others are weak.

Often we do not understand, as Abraham did, that as we struggle to overcome our human frailties, we gain true spirituality.

Coming To Terms With Who We Really Are

Coming to terms with who we really are leads to corrective action. It leads us to clean our house of our dark side without remorse. If we take responsibility for ourselves and our shortcomings, there are no bad feelings as long as we take corrective action.

For example, this is why there is no shame attached to saying that one is a recovering alcoholic for people in AA. This is because they are working on themselves to transform their negative traits into positive ones, in order to create lives based on forgiveness and love.

This is why there is no shame in admitting to ourselves that we come from homes with alcoholism and other problems, some of which others saw, and many of which were kept hidden. For we are now actively working on understanding and changing these legacies of the past and creating new traditions.

Two Of Our Masks — Perfection And Helplessness

We begin now by facing our dark side. We begin by identifying the survival masks that we learned to wear. These masks covered our true essence, and for this we paid a price. But these are also masks from which we gained, masks that allowed us to make a life for ourselves, to survive, and at times, to secretly grow. These are the masks that protected us.

Our Mask Of Perfection

For people who were brought up in alcoholic or traumatic homes, our self-esteem has become involved in creating a false mask of perfection for the world. From wearing this mask, we become compulsively self-reliant for we do not believe others could love us if they knew the side we keep hidden, the side of ourselves where we hide our jealousies, pettiness, greed and revengefulness. So we invest great energy in being perfect, to protect ourselves and to protect others from our dark side. And since we are "perfect", we feel that we are complete unto ourselves, and that we do not need others.

From our mask of perfection we often gain a feeling of power, of being better than others and therefore having some worth, however privately we kept this feeling. From perfectionism we also gain a facade of control. Our perfectionism can make us look as if we have it all together.

From our mask of perfectionism we stand as judge of all around us. We become critical and impossible to please. We stay on the offensive, constantly correcting everyone around us, keeping them busy looking at themselves, all so they won't criticize us. And we act confused when people rebel at our constant badgering. We explain how we were only trying to help them. And we really believe that we were trying to help. Not realizing that our perfectionism is a mask put on in fear.

Our Mask Of Helplessness

Another response to growing up in an alcoholic home is to develop a mask of helplessness, of compulsive dependence. We believe that we will be rejected if we are assertive or competent. So we cleverly create a face to show the world of a helpless, dependent individual.

We do this directly by appearing needy, when we secretly know that we are not. In fact we often resent being given to, for although we ask for help, we know that we do not need it.

Or we appear needy more indirectly. We hide behind this mask by taking care of others, compulsively, dependently, as a way of indirectly taking care of ourselves. We fear that we will not exist unless someone needs us, and we communicate this to others. Although we offer, we also resent others saying yes to our generosity, for we fear that our generosity will not be reciprocated. And yet we keep offering, and keep encouraging others to be dependent on us.

A Way Of Hiding

When we wear the mask of helplessness, it is because we have come to believe that being competent and autonomous will lead to rejection by our family and so we hide our assertiveness, real sexuality and leadership of our inner child.

But from our mask of helplessness we gain a sense of being loved. We gain an end to our isolation, for we have encouraged others to either care for us or depend on us. However we have arranged for others to be in our lives, we feel a connection to others, and from this connection, however ethereal it is or expensive to us it becomes, we derive hope.

The Price We Pay: An Inner World Of Fear And Self-Judgment

When we use either mask, when we go into hiding from the parts of ourselves we do not like, when we reject our totally lovable and imperfect inner child, we create an inner world of fear and self-judgment, where there should have been unconditional love and self-acceptance.

Until we learn differently, we continue to wear these masks in our adult life. The result is that the shame and rejection we experienced as children, if continued, can easily become self-hate, and as a result become part of our adult identity.

This is perhaps the saddest fact of all, for in attempting to protect ourselves, we begin to deny and eventually lose sight of our true self, our inner child, In fact, some of us will come to despise the vulnerable nature of our inner child as a sign of personal weakness.

Our Shield: Mind-Racing

You may be asking yourself why someone as sensitive and as tuned into their environment as we are would not know that we are wearing masks? The reason is that we have a shield against this knowledge, *mind-racing.* Mind-racing is constantly playing back different scenarios in our minds, different possibilities of what could have been or what could be. We do this to avoid the pressure and pain of the present. A major self-taught technique that has become for us a major energy drain, mind-racing is our ongoing attempt to control the past, the future and the present. It is our perfect escape for it is something that we are totally in control of.

Mind-racing is one of the most poignant ways that adult children have found to distract ourselves from the knowledge that we are in hiding; from the knowledge that we are wearing a mask; from the knowledge that we have a dark side; from the knowledge that we are feeling. Because it works so well, mind-racing becomes our shield against any new feeling or thought that threatens to challenge our careful, yet fragile system of self-protection.

A Learned Reaction

As adult children of alcoholics we had to find ways to control life around us. We learned, and in some instances taught ourselves, survival techniques. And once we found something that worked, we were reluctant to give it up, even when it cost us more to continue it than we gained from using it.

. . . To Stress

Thus a tool like mind-racing becomes our traditional reaction to any stress. Mind-racing becomes both our punishment and our reward. We punish ourselves by "mind-racing" — a pain we are in control of, a pain we have felt so often that we know exactly how to inflict it upon ourselves.

And we reward ourselves with mind-racing. It is a pain that is comforting due to its familiarity. It is a pain that we know that we can bear. And so we invite it, a known pain designed to block out any new pain.

A Major Energy Drain That Keeps Us In Crisis

We learned that if in our mind we kept playing back the event, real or imagined, we would almost feel that we could control it. Be it Dad coming home violent and drunk when we were seven, or our lover's most recent hurtful act. Over and over and over we play the same tape. We daydream about it. These thoughts would crowd our productive hours at work. We would think about these events during dinner. We would conjure these images during love-making, effectively limiting our pleasure. They even invade our dreams. Here our internal monologue turns to nightmares.

And yet, as painful as this process is we somehow feel it is worthwhile. Often we feel that playing out these worst case scenarios will help us, will strengthen us. We now know that we can face the worst. In fact, we keep practicing facing the worst, using a great part of our energy preparing for the worst, only to find ourselves drained and having little energy to implement any of our well-designed plans.

And so we go down the same road time and time again. We meet the same obstacles, feel the same overwhelming fear or rage and find ourselves at the same painful destination. We gain nothing by this repetition. But like loyal soldiers marching into a battle where we smell defeat, we go and go and go again. Like rats who have been trained to run the maze, run we do, until we begin to wonder why. Why are we shielding ourselves from being in the present?

A Defense Against Being Hurt

What we call character defects or negative traits or our dark side — our masks and our shield are really our childhood defenses against being hurt. They are the earliest way our inner child, deprived of his Higher Parent, made sense of the world. Our defenses represent how our inner child learned to protect himself from what felt at times to be a hostile environment.

Our defenses were developed by our inner child as ways of surviving the attacks that he felt upon his self-esteem. They developed as ways to ward off the reality of the pain of rejection, the fear of the unknown, the awareness of our dependence and vulnerability. They developed as ways to live in an initially unpredictable environment while maintaining self-esteem.

. . . That Also Maintains Integrity

It seemed so wise to develop these defenses. They made life livable, they gave us control, and they preserved our sense of integrity. And even if we paid a price for having these defenses, we often felt that we did get the better of the bargain, for we were able to survive and perhaps even to thrive, if only a little.

Our Oldest Friends

As a result, many of our defenses are really our oldest friends — tried and true. They have stood by us, protected us when all else failed. And even though now they do us little good, we are reluctant to discard them. Old defenses are sometimes like an old car which has served us well, been reliable and even fun, but is now breaking down. Like an old car, when the cost of the repair bills become more expensive than new monthly payments, we are still not able to sell it. So we keep it on the road to ward off the greater loss, the greater pain of parting with it.

This is also the way that many of us treat our childhood defenses. Although we are attached to them, although we know them, although we may even love them and respect them (we tend to be loyal, if nothing else), they may now be taking more from us than they give, even if in the past they were our best protectors. And yet we may still have difficulty in developing new defenses for we feel that we are rejecting our oldest friends.

Part Of Our Identity

Perhaps also, we are reluctant to acquire new defenses for we are not sure who we would be without our exclusive use of our old ones. They have been with us so long, they are part of our identity. After all, isn't part of how we see ourselves as always the one to give and not receive? Always the right one, even if we keep our rightness a secret? And what are these beliefs if not defenses in disguise?

Recovery Is About Self-Esteem

For recovery to take place we need to expand how we will protect ourselves. This does not mean giving up what has worked in the past. Loss is a very real issue for many adult children of alcoholics and other adult children of trauma. Recovery is not about more loss. Expanding our defenses means adding new defenses, new resources built on a more complete understanding of who we are and what we need.

Expanding our defenses means that we can also keep the old ones, even if we choose never to use them again. We do not have to discard them; they can be kept in the back of the closet of our defenses, ready for use if we choose, or to serve as a reminder of how we once protected ourselves.

Simply stated, as adults we need to have adult defenses.

This is not a benign world. Bad things do happen to good people. We do need to know how to protect ourselves. With maturity and knowledge we can now allow our Higher Parent to guide us to help defend us in ways that nourish us, in ways that are for our ultimate good.

Working Through The Pain

In order for real recovery to take place we must acknowledge and work through the original hurt our inner child experienced. This will be different for each of us. It may have been the issue of abandonment or the fear caused by violent parental eruptions, physical abuse, incest, being an immigrant, the child of a Holocaust survivor or the pitting of brother against sister. Our pain will probably have many sources. As we learned in Step 3, this is a tall order.

Soft Pain

Most of us spend our life trying to avoid feeling pain of childhood. We evade it with all kinds of diversions. We secretly fear we will not survive if we come into contact with that pain again. We fear becoming immobilized by the pain and not being able to take care of ourselves.

. . . Is The Path

This is exactly what a child living in an alcoholic home feels like, which is why many children of alcoholics will shut down their feelings. At the age of six, seven or eight those feelings were overwhelming. Our inner child knows this and fights to maintain survival at all costs. The first aim of childhood is to survive. Our inner child does not understand the difference between hard and soft pain.

. . . To Healing

Our Higher Parent will need to guide our inner child in knowing that we can go beyond survival. Our Higher Parent needs to help our inner child give in to the soft pain of healing. Our Higher Parent needs to let the child know that his old defenses are not needed and that he can survive this pain, and in fact he will be healed. But the first step in letting go of childhood defenses is to acknowledge and own them.

Stopping The Race — Using *Stop Thinking* — The Shield Antidote

In order to put aside our childhood trauma and embrace the fuller range of life's potentials, we need to be able to clear our thinking and to tell ourselves to stop.

We can learn new ways of thinking, new ways of handling old situations. We can learn to control our compulsive self-reliance and our negative obsessive thinking, our "mind-racing" by learning to say STOP, as a command, to ourselves and then feel the energy we have released within us.

Stop Thinking is a powerful tool that is developed by practicing. Certainly life gives us many opportunities to practice, so we don't have to worry about a good new tool and no place to use it.

By using Stop Thinking we will stop the learned self-flagellation, and replace it with love, acceptance and spontaneity.

Coming To Terms With Who You Are . . . Taking Stock

Taking stock of ourselves is a difficult task as we are taught to hide from our negative traits and ignore our positive traits. Thus making an inventory of our strengths and weaknesses is a frightening challenge!

Our Light Side: Strengths From Our Childhood

There are many positive traits that one develops growing up in an alcoholic or traumatized home. All too often we do not give ourselves credit for those strengths from childhood. Some of these are:

Self-Reliance. Many of us can attribute our resourceful-ness and self-reliance to our childhood struggles. In being forced to fend for ourselves we learned that we could take care of our needs, even if we did it awkwardly or inexpertly. We learned that we could and we did.

Compassion. For most of us our ability to have compas-sion for others stems from our experience as children growing up in traumatic families. From these experiences we have a great well of compassion, an abundance of empathy, which many others have difficulty in achieving. This compassion can be a main force in forging lasting relationships.

Empathy. Our ability to empathize with others is certainly one of our strengths, often it is seen in our choice of going into one of the helping professions, such as alcoholism or drug counselor, teacher, social worker, doctor, psychologist, nurse, member of the clergy or other professional fields where our main purpose is to serve others.

Leadership. Because we had to make it, often on our own, we learned that we could rally our resources. Often this made us stand out in school or at work, and we were looked up to as leaders. We were and often still are seen as being able to command attention and often respect.

Loyalty. We are loyal. Our loyalty can be at times our Achilles heel. We feel we must 'fight to the death' for a friend or loved one. We will not reject others, even when this may be necessary for us to move on with our life. Our loyalty allows us to stay with our families and friends through whatever adversity may befall them.

High Tolerence for Stress. This is a good news and bad news strength. We often tolerate high levels of ambiguity and uncertainty, for this is what we came to accept as normal as children. This strength makes us resilient as adults, as long as we do not crave stress and crisis in order to prove our worth to ourselves and others.

Positive Strengths From Childhood

If you think about it, you will find many more positive traits stemming from your childhood. We need to remember that growing up in alcoholic and similarly troubled homes made us more sensitive and aware than the average person. This is often the part of ourselves that we like the most.

Making An Inventory

Making a self-inventory is really giving an honest assessment of oneself, no better or worse than you really are. Making a self-inventory is essential to learning how to parent your inner child. Without an understanding of our defenses, we will not be able to transform them. Without an understanding of our strengths, we won't be able to maximize them.

First Steps

The best way to do an inventory is with a pencil and paper and a positive frame of mind. How do we begin?

Look At Your Dark Side

It is necessary to be specific about your childhood defenses, to make an inventory of your negative traits with a goal to understanding why you use them. By doing this, you are able to take steps to create alternatives.

Write down your negative traits in one column and across from them write down how they serve to protect your inner child. As you do this, you will identify areas where you will need to free your inner child. It will create a pattern. The following are some traits that you may relate to. Feel free to add others to make this truly your self-inventory.

Dark Side Trait	Way It Protects Me
I am judgmental	allows me to feel superior and avoid feeling insecure
I am disorganized	keeps me in crisis and able to avoid making necessary life changes
I am self-critical	allows me to avoid getting close to others and stay in constant pursuit of perfection

As you identify the ways you protect yourself, you will be able to have more compassion for your dark side and understand your goal to allow your Higher Parent to guide your inner child. You will be able to do this out of an inner direction born of love.

Identifying the areas where you protect yourself, will give you a road map for clarifying the areas which create the most amount of tension and require the most amount of love and self-acceptance. Accepting these areas allows us to venture gently into new ways to offer our inner child protection.

Then Look At Your Light Side

Acknowledge your strengths from childhood. Remember, children of alcoholics also gather many strengths and positive qualities from their childhood. It is important to recognize these. It is important to identify with our pluses as well as our minuses. It is important to remember that nothing, including ourselves, is all bad or all good.

Next write down your positive qualities — your light side attributes — and across from them write how they enhance your self-esteem. As you do this, you will identify positive alternatives, light side traits, that your Higher Parent can teach your inner child to use. This, too, will create a pattern.

Light Side Trait	Way It Enhances Me
I acknowledge when I am frightened	Allows me to drop my mask of perfection and feel secure in my real feelings
I am responsible and follow through	I feel I am a productive person and I am ending my family tradition of irresponsibility
I often acknowledge when I make mistakes	I feel more able to accept my own and other's imperfections and feel my love instead of my self-righteousness

As you identify the manner in which you enhance your self-esteem you will develop a road map. This map will lead you to ways of transforming your childhood defenses into behaviors that will serve to validate you as a person and create a world filled with love instead of fear.

There Is No Shame In Struggling

Like Abraham we all struggle. Remember there is no shame in being human. For Adult Children of Alcoholics (ACoAs) this is hard to accept. But once you admit to yourself that you are like everyone else, no better or worse, then you will find your real path to freedom. It is necessary to feel the pain of our childhood so that we can be free of the burden of the past and let go of old ways of living that are of no use to us anymore. Understanding that we develop defenses as a way of avoiding the pain of our childhood is integral to our future growth and development.

We are all imperfect. Our true worth is not gauged by how close to perfect we are, but by our struggle to overcome our imperfections. We are no better or worse than anyone else. If we understand that our inner child is frightened and hurt and protects himself, then there is nothing to be ashamed of when we give over to our dark side. It is simply our inner child reminding us how frail and human we are.

As long as we try to understand why our inner child had chosen the defenses he has and when to add adult to old childhood defenses, recovery will be ours.

Each of us wonders if there is more in life, more for us. And, yes, we do perhaps feel a little crazed as we question old loyalties, old friends. And we do feel pain as we separate from what we knew, and sail away to new horizons, new ways of being, new ways of allowing ourselves to feel and new ways of protecting ourselves.

But if we are clear on our goal of allowing our Higher Parent to guide us, then we can have our needs met in new ways. We will be able to be in the world without hiding, without masks, no longer ashamed of ourselves for being human and having frailties. We will be able to face the world with self-confidence and self-respect. We will be able to create ways of being in the world that will increase self-esteem, rather than diminish us. We, too, will be able to fulfill ourselves, fulfill our inner child. When we see the things we want, we will be able to take the things we see, without guilt or shame or in hiding but as free self-affirming individuals!

Setting The Stage To Welcome — The Real You

Our real goal in life is to transform our negative traits into positive loving traits, which will enable us to free our inner child and release the God force, our Higher Parent in each of us.

Many of us think we are only our dark side and that the loving and caring things we do are only momentary victories over our dark side. Most of us do not identify with the positive forces within us. We do not identify with the divinity within us connecting us to one another and to all living things in the universe. We do not see ourselves as we really are, children of the one great oneness, struggling to express itself through us as the ultimate force of love and abundance.

Meditations On Parenting Your Inner Child

Know that your real self is full of love and self-acceptance. Know that at your core you are full of love and forgiveness. Accept that all of your negative traits only serve to cloud your love for your inner child. Know that your negative traits are a defense developed in childhood. Treat yourself, therefore, with compassion, rather than criticism when you encounter a defense on your road to recovery.

Fear nothing, neither lack, limitation, disappointment nor distress of any kind. Know that you no longer need to hide from your dark side traits. Accept yourself and commit yourself to ever unfolding as a child of the light. Take a self-inventory in order to understand who you really are. Do this in order to come to terms with your assets and deficits while practicing self-acceptance, viewing yourself all the while in the forgiving light of love and self-acceptance. Accept that your childhood hurts are being healed right now by a healing light which surrounds you. Acknowledge the specific areas of your life where you are frightened. Witness this fear dissipating as your inner light illuminates each dark corner of your consciousness.

Realize that you have the power to control your thoughts. Lovingly exercise this power to stop negative unproductive thinking. Recognize the need to guide your inner child by using your Higher Parent to teach him new ways to see the world. Forgive yourself and embrace yourself with a healing light.

Daily Self-Parenting Affirmations

I acknowledge that I am a child of light and that my true nature is one of love not fear.

I acknowledge my right to be a happily successful person. I acknowledge my responsibility to myself to support the best in myself while working to transform the worst.

I am guided in everything I do by a greater consciousness than my own.

I acknowledge that I am a child of love. I acknowledge my true nature. I am connected to all living things through my divine nature.

I am no longer bound by mistakes of the past. I free myself to live in the present and to trust in the future.

CHAPTER 5

Intimacy: Your Inner Child's Connection To The Outer World

A.A. Step 5: Admitted to God, to ourselves, and to another human being the exact nature of our wrongs.

Self-Parenting Step 5: Learned to share our self-parenting issues with others without self-recrimination or shame.

"For each of us there is only one path out of shame, to let the love of a child wash over our hearts and give us direction . . . towards self-acceptance."

Anonymous from an ACoA

"No se puede vivir sin amour . . . (It is not possible to live without love.)

*"The Consul", from **Under The Volcano** by Malcolm Lowry*

Love

Unqualified love is the core of your inner child. The child seeks to give and receive love, and by doing this achieves intimacy with others. As the child grows, the child learns that love is not always accepted or returned. For people who have grown up in alcoholic or traumatic families, the child often learns that love is dangerous.

As we grow older, we learn to hide the true nature of our inner child from others. Eventually we even hide it from ourselves. In an effort to protect the vulnerability of our inner child, we mask our love and deprive ourselves of the ability to achieve intimacy. In time we forget how to take the mask off.

Intimacy

Intimacy is the way we share ourselves with the people we trust. It is the most basic form of validation that we have. Without intimacy we are lost and isolated and cannot thrive. Instead of being taught how to create healthy intimacy with others, many of us had been taught to fear others, to make intimate contact through conflict and crisis and to hide our need for support and help.

Having grown up in families where secrecy is the primary rule and perfectionism the primary goal, we often have no healthy role models for developing honest and open relationships. Many of us grow up thinking that showing love is a sign of weakness. Needing anything, especially intimacy, is an invitation to be attacked or humiliated. We see a loving parent being rejected by a withholding parent and we assume that the withholding parent is stronger and does not need love or intimacy. We draw the conclusion that the need for intimacy and love is weakness, withholding love and intimacy is strength.

Shame For Loving And Intimacy

We become ashamed of our need for love and intimacy. We become ashamed of our spiritual feelings because they bring us in touch with our love for God. The belief that showing love is weak removes us from our spiritual center and shuts us off from intimate contact with our Higher Parent and our inner child.

On the deepest level we fear that loving will make us weak and helpless. It is a defense from childhood that we needed when we could not tolerate the truth that our love was often rejected by our parents because it tapped into their fear of their own vulnerability. It is a defense that our Higher Parent can guide us to let go of so that our inner light can shine forth in its true loving nature.

Shame For Living

For adult children of alcoholics shame has another meaning. It is the backdrop for our approach to life. We feel shame about our families. We feel shame for having failed to save our parents from themselves. We feel shame for not being able to exist without help from others. In short we feel shame about most of our life!

Shaming is something that adults do to children and children learn to do to themselves. Shaming is about humiliation. It is about devaluation of self. Unfortunately in most addicted families shaming and humiliation are the chief tools used for controlling children.

Shame inhibits life. It makes love and intimacy impossible. It imprisons our inner child in a cage of self-hate. The inner child feels that she is a failure because she was not perfect and feels responsible for the dysfunction in her family. It is old baggage that needs to be discarded. It is necessary for our Higher Parent to teach our inner child to let go of this destructive attitude.

Sharing . . . The Way Out Of Shame

The way out of shame is to break the silence about ourselves. We need to allow our Higher Parent to teach our inner child to share ourselves, our feelings and our self-parenting issues with others. We must learn to share our dark side and our light side traits with one another. We need to learn that who we are is not just the trauma and unhappiness of our childhood but all of it, good and bad. We need to learn to share all of who we are if we are to achieve true intimacy. Our Higher Parent can help us with this.

We need to use our Higher Parent to teach our inner child that it is safe to share who we really are and vital to our well-being to break the silence.

This will feel wrong at the beginning because talking to others is breaking with your family tradition of secrecy. Sharing with others creates a new tradition of trust and guilt-free living. Sharing your self-parenting issues with others is a way of opening your heart to the world and admitting that you are not perfect and that you are worthwhile just as you are.

Without Recrimination

Guilt is the great divider. It separates us from each other. It is also a way of keeping the focus on ourselves. When we hurt someone and feel guilt instead of sorrow, we are not truly sorry for what we have done.

Self-recrimination is a way of shutting people out and staying stuck in ourselves. Guilt is all about us, how bad we are, how insensitive we are, etc. and not about others. It does not concern itself with the feelings of others.

And Sometimes With Feeling Sorrow

When we do something hurtful to others and we feel the pain we have caused someone else, then we feel sorrow for our actions. Sorrow is taking responsibility with your feelings for the pain you have caused. Sorrow does not devalue you like guilt and shame do. Sorrow allows you to feel your pain, and the pain of others.

When we feel sorrow for what we have done, we don't beat up on ourselves. We see and feel the result of our behavior and we change the behavior. Sorrow is about taking responsibility and changing. Guilt and self-recrimination is about wallowing in self-pity, and holding on to old ways of thinking and behaving. Feeling sorrow is about feeling the pain of others.

When we share with others without self-recrimination, we allow for real communication to take place. When we share with our feelings, we can leave the baggage of the past behind. We can admit the exact nature of our wrongs and let go of them. When we share without self-recrimination, we open ourselves up to the greater community of humanity.

Trust Your Heart

Our hearts are our best teachers. For adult children of alcoholics the heart is the hardest thing to trust. We have been trained to trust our heads, to reason, to sort things, not to feel our way through life.

If we are to be whole people, vulnerable and able to give and receive love, we must learn to trust our heart and let it lead the way, trusting in our Higher Parent to protect us as we go. If we are ever to enter the world in all our fullness to reach for the stars and let our dreams of intimacy come true, we must become as children full of love and full of heart. In this way our Higher Parent will teach and protect our inner child to trust appropriately to share herself with her sisters and brothers and to follow the best life has to offer.

Meditations On Parenting Your Inner Child

Know that unqualified love is the core of your inner child. Know that your true nature is love. Know that intimacy is your inner child's connection to the outer world. Imagine yourself letting go of all your masks and letting your true core shine true as a child of the light.

Allow your Higher Parent to reassure your inner child that loving is strength. Challenge your belief that showing love is a sign of weakness. Challenge your fear that if you surrender to your heart, you will become helpless and at the mercy of others. Allow your Higher Parent to comfort your inner child and to discover her true power and strength.

Allow yourself to feel the pain you have caused other people, without judging yourself. Visualize someone you have hurt in front of you in your mind's eye. Open your heart to them, feel their pain and ask for forgiveness. Know that at the moment of sincere asking, you are forgiven. Feel your commitment to change hurtful behavior.

Bring the world into your heart. Visualize yourself welcoming someone you like into your heart. Visualize your heart as a welcoming home where you and all you invite in are safe. Next visualize yourself inviting someone you don't like into your heart. Let your love wash over both of you and bless you in a greater consciousness. Know that this greater consciousness is the divinity within you, the spark of God in all of us. Commit yourself to this oneness and know that this is who you really are.

Daily Self-Parenting Affirmations

I know that my heart is my best teacher. I commit myself to following my heart's lead, allowing my Higher Parent to guide me along the way.

I acknowledge that my real strength comes from my ability to love and trust, not from my ability to perform. I affirm that as I open up to others, I increase my real power and show my real strength.

I welcome the opportunity to share my real self with others and join in the community of person-hood, no better or worse than anyone else.

I allow myself to feel the pain I have caused others. I do not judge myself for this. I accept responsibility for the harm I have done others and commit myself to change behaviors which are hurtful to others.

CHAPTER 6

Overcoming Perfectionism

A.A. Step 6: Were entirely ready to have God remove all these defects of character.

Self-Parenting Step 6: Became ready to change by giving up the demand to be perfect.

The Birthmark

In the latter part of the last century there lived a man of science, an eminent scholar proficient in every branch of natural philosophy, who . . . persuaded a beautiful woman to become his wife . . . One day, very soon after their marriage, Aylmer sat gazing at his wife with a trouble on his countenance that grew . . .

"Georgiana," said he, "has it never occurred to you that the mark upon your cheek might be removed?"

"No, indeed," said she . . ."To tell you the truth it has been so often called a charm that I was simple enough to imagine it might be so."

"Ah, upon another face perhaps it might," replied her husband, "but never on yours . . . you came so nearly perfect . . . that this slightest possible defect . . . shocks me."

. . . Georgiana soon learned to shudder at his gaze.

"Aylmer," resumed Georgiana solemnly one day, "I know not what may be the cost to both of us to rid me of this fatal birthmark . . . If there is the remotest possibility of it . . . let the attempt be made at whatever the risk."

. . . Her husband tenderly kissed her cheek — her right cheek — not that which bore the impress of the crimson hand.

The next day Aylmer apprised his wife of a plan . . . He bore a crystal goblet containing a liquor colorless as water, but bright enough to be the draught of immortality.

Observed his wife, "Life is but a sad possession to those who have attained precisely the degree of moral advancement at which I stand. Were I weaker and blinder, it might be happiness. Were I stronger, it might be endured hopefully. But being what I find myself, me thinks I am of all mortals the most fit to die."

She quaffed the liquid and returned the goblet to his hand.

"My peerless bride, it is successful! You are perfect!". . .

"My poor Aylmer," she repeated with more than human tenderness, "Do not repent that with so light and pure a feeling, you have rejected the best the earth could offer. Dearest Aylmer, I am dying!"

As the last crimson tint of the birthmark — that sole human imperfection — faded from her cheek, the parting breath of the now perfect woman passed into the atmosphere, and her soul, lingering a moment near her husband, took its heavenward flight . . ."

Excerpted from a short story, **The Birthmark** by Nathaniel Hawthorne

The Seduction Of Perfectionism

We all have our "birthmarks", those qualities that are imperfect within us. These are also the qualities which make each of us unique. This knowledge and acceptance of our differences are understood by our Higher Parent. Acceptance of "birthmarks", our imperfections, our uniqueness, be they visible or invisible, is how we accept ourselves. When we choose to reject a part of ourselves, even one of our "birthmarks", then we court the type of disaster depicted in the story.

The price paid for the striving for perfection is death. It is a death of our spirit, of our specialness, of what we can offer, which is uniquely ours to give. It is the death of our inner child.

To be imperfect is to be human. To dwell on our imperfections, as Aylmer does, is to miss the beauty that does exist. He failed to ". . . find the perfect future in the present", for he dwelled on what needed to be changed, not what was there to enjoy.

To have flaws is to be alive, our differences give us our identity. They keep us striving and risking; they comprise the curiosity of our inner child. Perfection is a quality of the gods alone — those beings who do not inhabit our sphere of consciousness.

The Need To Be Perfect

Yet despite the obvious pain of our quest for perfection, one of our most commonly used defenses is perfectionism. The goal of perfectionism would be worth working towards, perhaps, if it could be reached. We could all work really hard, deny ourselves, risk a type of death and at least at the end of it, we could say, "Well, I suffered but at least my child had the perfect life" or "I had the perfect career, even if I've not had a social life" or "My husband's career advanced, even if I have no identity outside of my home." Then there would have been some reason for the sacrifices. We could console ourselves by saying that even though we lost our child, our spouse, our mother or father, sister or brother who we loved so much, we still gained.

"I sacrificed, but it was worth it."

Except this isn't what happens. Our trying to be perfect for ourselves or for another, does not advantage them, it only disadvantages us.

Perfection's Not-So-Hidden Payoff

Life Is Simple

You may be wondering why someone, maybe even you, would want to be perfect? Trying to be perfect has a wonderful payoff. It keeps life black or white. Very simple. Everything is in its nice neat package. And if it is not white, then it is black and hopeless. Striving for perfectionism keeps us from living with the anxiety and ambiguity of the world of grey.

If perfection is our goal, our payoff may be that we do not have to work very hard, for we unconsciously know that our goal is beyond us. This subconscious knowledge can protect us from really risking ourselves. As bad as it feels, being perfectionistic could be protecting us from feeling even worse.

We Do Not Have To Own How We Feel

Perfectionism is also a convenient smoke screen for our feelings. We learn to do and not to feel. Our inner child cannot grow. Our feelings of mastery, how our inner child learns, are thwarted by depending on something or someone else, instead of learning to depend on ourselves, on our Higher Parent and inner child.

The Best Excuse To Do Nothing Risky

Perfectionism also sets a standard for achievement that is so high, that on some level no one has to try to achieve it, for we know that it is beyond us. Having the goal of perfectionism is, therefore, a good excuse to do nothing. It keeps us focused on ourselves and on our own shortcomings and protects us from encouraging and confronting ourselves and others to change.

We Can Be Defined By Others

When we let others define us, tell us who we are and what we should do as did Georgiana in the story, then we are continuing our family tradition of compulsive dependency.

With compulsive dependency we are defined from the outside. We learn to invalidate feelings and aspirations that come from the inside, that come from our inner child. With compulsive dependency we invalidate our Higher Parent. We learn not to check into ourselves for guidance. As a result we learn to be dependent upon someone else, something else to fulfill us, to validate us, to give us meaning.

When our goal is perfectionism, then we are allowing an arbitrary standard to tell us what we must do. We do not listen to the voice of our inner child, the voice of love, nor do we counsel with our Higher Parent, the voice of reason. We pay homage instead to the voices which teach us to be helpless. We learn to compulsively eat, drink, drug, shop, gamble, work, have compulsive sexual intercourse.

We Can Be Safe From Intimacy

When we judge ourself as imperfect and therefore unworthy, we have the perfect excuse (no pun intended) to not be vulnerable. We do not have to risk being open to finding someone with whom we can trust enough to have intimacy. We can continue our family's tradition of compulsive self-reliance and let no one touch us.

Perfectionism's Expense

When looked at this way, perfectionism becomes a very expensive way to feel good. And an even more expensive way to feel safe. There are many other ways to feel protected, but they involve freeing your Higher Parent to protect your inner child. The world will suddenly seem much more complicated and perhaps even more frightening. And new ways will need to be learned to have your "force", your Higher Parent, protect you. So if you are ready to consider changing, begin by getting ready.

The Price Of Change

Change is scary. Change needs to be prepared for. Too often we try to throw ourselves into a different behavior, only to be overwhelmed by the fact that we cannot do it all at once. And so we give up feeling that we are doomed to repeat the mistakes of our past for change is beyond us.

Change is frightening for it means inviting in the unknown. Once we spin the wheel of change, we can never be sure of where we will land. This is why we need to prepare ourselves for change, slowly and gently. The process of preparing for change is the work of the 6th Step.

Since change can be overwhelming, it is natural to resist it, to find reasons, good reasons, why it is not possible. By resisting, we protect ourselves. And protecting ourselves isn't a bad goal, is it? In fact much of our behavior can be seen as self-protective. Self-protective behaviors are also called defenses. And we all need defenses as we saw in the work of the 4th Step. The goal of the Twelve Steps of self-parenting is certainly not to be defenseless in the world.

Becoming Ready To Give Up
What Does Not Work

This is not a benign world; terrible and unfair things do happen to each of us. We do need to learn to take care of ourselves. Our defenses are one of the ways that the inner child in us protects us. Many defenses will work well in this world.

But we need to understand that some of our defenses are or can be dysfunctional. They presently take more from us than they give, even if in the past they were our best protectors, our very best friends.

As we saw in the work of the 4th Step, some of our old defenses drain energy from us. They do not protect us now as they once did. In fact some of our defenses may do us real harm by allowing us to have unrealistic expectations. Perfectionism is one of these defenses.

In beginning to get ready to change what does not work, we need to realize that we are only contemplating adding on ways for our inner child to protect us, not giving up ways that have worked.

The work of this step is to begin to set the stage for change by giving up the defense of perfectionism. We cannot change if our goal is perfection. Perfectionism gives us no place to go. It keeps us merely stuck.

Owning Our Power — Actively Employing Our Higher Parent

To think about change we need to do only one simple task and this is to own our power, the knowledge of our intuitive and present Higher Parent. We have great power over how we choose to live our life and over how we choose to protect our inner child. We have so much power that it can be frightening, which may be why we choose to pretend that we have less knowledge of ourselves than indeed we do. In preparing to change, all we need to do now is to consider how we want things to be.

As Yogi Desai says, "You are the creator. Whatever you think, that is what you create, and that is what you become."

The work of this step is to own our power to create ourselves.

Meditations On Parenting Your Inner Child

Surrender yourself to your Higher Parent and your God to guide you. Know that by surrendering you pave the way to change.

Allow yourself to begin your journey of change. Accept that change is frightening. Know that you have all that you need within yourself to change.

Be gentle with yourself. Prepare for change by inviting it. Prepare for change by gathering support from your Higher Parent, your Higher Power and energy from your inner child.

Know that you will always be who you are. No magnitude of change can alter your true essence if you allow yourself to be guided from within. Allow that when you give up the need to be perfect, you will be more of who you always were.

Daily Self-Parenting Affirmations

I am complete just the way I am.

I have the power to claim all of me.

I can and will depend upon myself to define me.

I love all of my parts, even the parts of myself that I do not understand.

I am perfect unto myself.

CHAPTER 7

Embracing Our Oneness:
Serenity, Joy And Belonging

A.A. Step 7: Humbly asked Him to remove our shortcomings.

Self-Parenting Step 7: Learned to embrace our uniqueness and connectedness to others in a spirit of love and humility.

Humility is just as much the opposite of self-abasement as it is of self-exaltation. To be humble is not to make comparisons. Secure in its reality, the self is neither better or worse, bigger nor smaller, than anything else in the universe. It is — is nothing, yet at the same time one with everything . . .
Towards this, so help me, God . . .

Dag Hammarskjold from **Markings**

We Are All Connected — Serenity

There is a central truth which we often forget: We, each of us, are connected one to the other. Regardless of the difference in our backgrounds or in our station in life, we are still equal in our humanness. All great religious philosophies have expressed the same essential relationship among all living things. And it is through humility that we experience our oneness with each other and the cosmos. It is through living a humble life that we learn we are a small part of a greater whole.

When we are humbly grounded the winds of success and adversity whirl around us without disturbing our center of serenity. A world of extraordinary wonders is now opened to us as we are cushioned in the unshakable security that comes from a feeling of connectedness to God and to humanity.

Comparing Disconnects Us From One Another — Belonging

Many of us were compared to siblings or other children by our parents. Often we may have been told that we were not as good as other children. This constant comparison between us and others led to a belief that the only way we could feel good about ourselves was to be better than someone else. This led to competition and a belief that life was a win/lose ballgame.

We came to believe that our only value in life was based on our ability to perform, first for our parents and later for loved ones and bosses. We fostered our compulsive self-reliance as a way of maintaining ourselves as separate and better than everyone else. And while many of us achieved a great deal in our chosen professions or as parents, our momentary self-esteem was always attached to our achievements and did not stem from our intrinsic value as people and children of God. Our self-esteem was attached to being better than someone else.

We Are No Better Or Worse Than Anyone Else

For adult children of alcoholics or other people who have lived in homes where the children had parental or unusual roles, we have grown up with the realization that somehow we are different. Many of us have raised our brothers and sisters. Some of us grew up and were made into substitute husbands or wives by our parents.

We have needed to become resourceful in order to survive our childhood. We had to develop skills that other people did not develop in order to get by each day. For instance, we are often more sensitive to our environment than other people are. We have learned to read other people's moods through their body language, which is why some of us believe that we are psychic. Or we become experts at dealing with crisis, which is why so many of us work in the helping professions.

These experiences and attributes all combine to create a feeling of uniqueness. Often we unconsciously and sometimes consciously feel superior to other people who have not gone through what we've gone through. We secretly believe that we are smarter and tougher and more resourceful than other people. We secretly believe that somehow our suffering has set us apart and made us better than other people. While it is true that we are unique in our experience, it is not true that our experience has made us better than other people.

We Learn To Value Intellect

Because adult children of alcoholics rely on their intellect to reason through the problems in their lives, often at the expense of their feelings, they learn to value intellect over feelings and feel intellectually superior to other people. This intellectual superiority is often expressed as cynicism or impatience with others who are not as bright as we are.

This sense of superiority is another attribute that sets us apart from others and creates a gulf which inhibits us from reaching real intimacy with others. The same traumatic childhood that we wanted to escape becomes a prison when we wear our struggles as a badge of honor on our chests. Our pride for surviving our childhood becomes the glue that sticks us in the past and keeps us from moving on with our lives.

Over Love

Instead of learning to self-parent ourselves in healthy ways through developing trust in others and nurturing our emotional well-being, we cling to the false belief that we are superior beings because we have learned to live without love and validation and a host of other necessary things.

We ignore our need for human contact or our need to be connected to the greater world. We try to live without feeling anything, especially love or pain. We wear our intellectual superiority as a mask which hides the frightened child inside.

Putting Ourselves Down Is An Act of Pride

There is an old saying that it is as much an act of pride to put yourself down as it is to build yourself up. In each case we are showing everyone how important we are. Real humility has been described as an honest assessment of yourself, no better or worse than you really are. This has often been misunderstood. Many of us think that by making ourselves out to be inferior we are acting humble. They do not understand that humility does not come from putting yourself down. Low self-esteem comes from putting yourself down.

Many of us were put down as children and learned to put ourselves down as a consequence. For some of us it is a natural response to point out to people what is wrong with us. We strive to point out what is wrong first, before the other sees it. People who are caught up in the web of self-deprecation will often use a job interview, for instance, as an opportunity to tell a prospective employer all the reasons not to hire them. Or they will tell a prospective mate all of their faults, their shortcomings, their previous missteps in life.

We put ourselves down as adults if our parents or family members put us down as children. For our inner child it is simply a way to maintain a family tradition. The inner child finds ways to stay loyal to his family, even if it means that his self-esteem is sacrificed in the bargain. Our Higher Parent needs to teach the inner child that being loyal in this way is not what we need to do.

God Does Not Make Junk

A lot of us were taught that to be proud of our achievements was a sin of pride and so we shunned our achievements and the applause that came with them. We constantly minimize all our successes. What we failed to realize is that while we were busy working so hard to minimize ourselves, we were maintaining the focus on ourselves, increasing our egotism, even as we diminished ourselves. So in the end nothing was gained by making ourselves out to be worse than other people, except the feelings of self-rejection and self-hate, which is the natural product of such behavior.

For most of us accepting that we are good people, not worse than others, is painful because it reminds us of how unfairly we were treated as children. To accept that God does not make junk is to accept that we are valuable as people, just the way we are and that the messages from childhood were wrong.

Real Humility

Real humility is achieved when we stop comparing ourselves to others and accept ourselves as we are. Our inner child needs to be guided by the Higher Parent in this area. He doesn't trust that he will be loved and valued unless the game of better or worse is continued. This is all the inner child knows.

Like all children the inner child truly believes that he is all powerful. Your Higher Parent will need to set limits on the inner child's false need to puff himself up or put himself down. When we let go of the need to compare ourselves to others, we let go of a great deal of unnecessary baggage. When we let go of the need to put others down, we let go of the fear that we will be diminished by the successes of others.

Embracing Our True Value — Joy

When we release ourselves from the resentment that comes from putting ourselves down in order to feel accepted by our family members, we accept a world where each of us is valued as a birthright, a world where you don't have to constantly be proving yourself in order to feel loved.

When we accept that different does not mean better, we move closer to our Higher Power and true brother and sisterhood with the family of man. When the burden of competition is removed from our shoulders, we are able to lift ourselves up, see the world as it really is and in the process discover true security . . . through the knowledge that we are perfect and lovable as we are.

By these simple acts we open up a world of wonder and peace where we see the commonality of things instead of the differences. Thus we are able to clear our vision of ego and move beyond our fight for survival into a new world of abundance and joy. When we embrace our oneness we can see the divinity within all things that is the source of all life.

It is not surprising that Dag Hammarskjold, who served for many years as Secretary-General of the United Nations, strived to live a humble life. He understood that only from a place of humility could he lead the nations of the world on the path of peace and unity. He understood that egotism breeds separation. He understood that the path of humility opens up vistas of a wondrous world hidden from view when we lose ourselves in egotism.

Recovery And Our Higher Parent

Practicing humility in your self-parenting will allow you to experience recovery on its most serene level. When we let go of the need to be better or worse, we leave behind the destructive competitiveness fostered in our distorted childhood, we release ourselves from the belief that in order to be loved and valued, we must keep out-achieving our fellows. When we embrace our oneness with the universe, we allow our Higher Parent to emerge.

It will be hard for us to let go of an opportunity to increase our self-importance. But our Higher Parent will help us to resist. Our Higher Parent can remind us that whether we build ourselves up or put ourselves down, we are complicating our lives. Our Higher Parent will remind us that all tasks are equal to God and nature. In this way we can learn to be who we are and claim all that we are, no more, no less, and derive the benefits of a humble life of serenity and joy and a true sense of belonging.

The Twelve Steps are a simple program for complicated people. Left to our own devices we will make difficult that which is easy. Life is a journey to be experienced, not a problem to be solved. Allowing our Higher Parent to teach our inner child the value of simple humble living will keep us untouched by the whirlwinds of success and adversity.

Meditations On Parenting Your Inner Child

Embrace your oneness with all living things. Visualize yourself connected to all living things by a ribbon of white light. Witness as simply one flower from the human bouquet. Let yourself experience the sense of belonging that comes from the reality of your relatedness to all living things.

Experience the reality that you are valuable and perfect just the way you are. Feel the serenity that comes from knowing you no longer have to compare and compete with others. Practice self-acceptance in everything you do. Know that there is no need to perform for your Higher Power. Let your Higher Parent comfort your inner child with this knowledge.

Visualize yourself living in a simple and humble fashion. Imagine yourself in a world where applause is not important, where each talent and each person is valued equally. Imagine a world where love is given freely as a birthright, and each of us is regarded without reference to our sex, the color of our skin or station in life. Know that each of us creates the world we live in and the world we invite others to live in with us. Commit yourself to creating a world of joy and hope. Know that as you think so shall it be.

Daily Self-Parenting Affirmations

I affirm my connectedness to all living things. I embrace the oneness which is the ultimate reality of life.

I accept that my uniqueness does not make me better or worse than anyone else. I affirm that I am lovable and valuable. I do not have to prove myself at the expense of others in order to feel validated.

I affirm who I am just as I am. I live each day claiming my successes and accepting my failures without losing or gaining self-esteem. I recognize my true value is my birthright and not something I must earn.

Learning Self-Forgiveness: Making Amends To Your Inner Child

A.A. Step 8: Made a list of all persons we had harmed, and became willing to make amends to them all.

Self-Parenting Step 8: Learned self-forgiveness and made amends to our inner child.

Our Love For Our Inner Child:
The Gateway To Self-Forgiveness

There was a certain Pharisee, who invited Jesus to dine with him. Jesus went to the Pharisee's home and reclined to eat. A woman known in the town to be a sinner learned that he was dining in the Pharisee's home. She brought in a vase of perfumed oil and stood behind him at his feet, weeping so that her tears fell upon his feet. Then she wiped them with her hair, kissing them and perfuming them with the oil. When his host, the Pharisee, saw this, he said to himself, "If this man were a prophet, he would know who and what sort of woman this is that touches him — that she is a sinner."

In answer . . . Jesus said, "You see this woman? I came to your home and you provided me with no water for my feet. She has washed my feet with her tears and wiped them with her hair. You gave me no kiss, but she has not stopped kissing my feet since I entered. You did not anoint my head with oil, but she has anointed my feet with her perfume. I tell you, that is why her many sins are forgiven — because of her great love."

Luke 7:36 — 8:47

Making Amends By Learning Forgiveness And
Self-Forgiveness

Making amends is not just saying, "I'm sorry." Certainly we need to acknowledge what we have done to another in order to learn from it, and in order to become willing to develop a new response. But true amends are about changing our life through learning to forgive ourselves and others. And forgiveness and self-forgiveness are about separating ourselves from our past.

Using Our Higher Parent To Learn — Forgiveness

Forgiveness may sound like an impossible dream to many who have been raised in families full of anger and hurt. Yet the ability to forgive is accessible to all of us if we allow ourself to be guided by our intuitive wisdom, our Higher Parent. This is the part of us that can see events as neutral and guide our inner child in understanding so that she will not judge another.

It is often our judgment of another's act as "harmful", "mean" or "spiteful" that causes the tension between us. Tension that is present when we see, think of or are reminded of the other person. Forgiveness is about releasing ourselves and others from this tension.

Judgments of another take time and energy. They fill us with rage in the place where there could be love. Forgiveness means making space within — for us to go on with our lives and not be consumed by the actions of another.

If we did not react, did not allow another to harm us, whatever they intended, or if we could see their action as their problem and not ours, there would be nothing to condemn them for. We could then ask only that they be released and hope that they would allow their Higher Parent to guide them.

Using Our Higher Parent To Learn — Self-Forgiveness

Luke tells us, "Forgive and we shall be forgiven" (6:37). Often to forgive ourselves we need to learn to forgive others. In releasing others from what they have done to us, we can begin to release ourselves from what we have done to ourselves and to others.

Self-blame takes up energy and time. When we blame ourselves, we center on ourselves. We literally make ourselves the center of the universe. We use our creative ability and our strength to keep recounting to ourselves our past deeds, which we wish we could take back. Deeds which are over, done and which no amount of desire, time or energy can undo. We keep ourselves stuck in a quagmire of self-blame.

We need to free ourselves from the mind-racing which keeps us in the past, which takes our energies and keeps us looking back with pain and torment. We need to free ourselves to be in the present, to be in this moment, to learn from this moment. And to love our inner child and others within this precious space.

If Mary Magdalene had been consumed by self-blame for her many sins, she would not have had the energy or desire to reach out with love to ask for forgiveness. Her asking for forgiveness was in part how Mary Magdalene loved her inner child, for by asking for forgiveness she was able to begin to forgive herself.

Sharing Love Will Heal Us

As we are told, it was her love that caused her to be forgiven. It was not a small love, but had the power to release all of her love to share. This is what allowed her to be healed. So too with us the love that our inner child has can heal us. When we stay in touch with our love for our inner child, then we will keep alive the power we have to forgive ourselves moment to moment, day to day.

Acknowledging The Impact Of Our Actions Frees Us

To forgive ourselves we need to release ourselves from our past deeds. This means that we need to acknowledge we have hurt others. Sometimes this may have been intentional. At other times this may have come about by our not being emotionally available to ourselves, resulting in hurting the other. So we have unintentionally hurt another. The result is the same, through our conscious or unconscious acts, others have suffered. We need to accept this, not only so we can make amends to them, but also so we can make amends to our inner child, who feels the pain we have caused others and cringes.

To forgive ourselves we need to use our Higher Parent to release ourselves from our judgment of our past deeds. It does no good to walk around keeping the shame alive. It does neither us nor anyone else any good to constantly feel that we have damaged our children or that our parents will never speak to us again or that our spouse is about to leave us.

It serves no purpose to retraumatize ourselves by constantly remembering those acts and words we wish we could take back. It keeps us immobilized and unable to take steps to improve our lives today.

Our Reactions Are A Mirror

We need to judge ourselves less and accept ourselves more to be able to do this with others. Part of our love for our inner child is to accept our actions, to allow our actions to be guided by our Higher Parent. After all, our reactions to others are but a mirror of our feelings about ourselves. Self-acceptance means taking responsibility for what we have done to others and to ourselves, not blaming ourselves. Self-acceptance means being honest about the impact of our actions and where we see change is needed, preparing to change.

Responsibility Without Guilt

Many of us confuse guilt with responsibility. For those of us who have had traumatic childhoods where we lived with abusive alcoholic or other troubled parents, there will be even more of a tendency to confuse the guilt and responsibility, as this is what we learned in our home.

Responsibility

Responsibility says, "I did it. If I hurt you, then I am sorry. And if I shouldn't have said or done what I did, then I shall try to make amends" (the work of the next Step). Responsibility leads to a reconciliation.

Responsibility means accepting the past for what it is and making a commitment to change some of your self-parenting strategies. Responsibility also means being specific about what we want to change. We cannot become different people nor do we need to be. We can instead become more fulfilled and complete. Sometimes changing some of the ways we act can make us more fulfilled and happier. We can be more of who we truly are. We can be more assured of ourselves by taking more responsibility for our actions.

Guilt

Guilt says, "I did something, and I should punish myself for it." Guilt focuses all of our energy on ourselves. With guilt we feel that we did something, we may not even be clear what it is, but we know we should punish ourselves for whatever it was.

Guilt is a one-way feeling. It is all about how we feel and not about how to make amends to the other. There is nothing in our guilt for the other person unless they feel better seeing us suffer (and if they do feel better as we feel worse, we need to clearly look at this relationship).

At times it often seems that our guilt shuts out the other person's feelings. Our guilt says, "If we punish ourselves, we do not have to deal with how hurt or angry the other is." The problem with our guilt is that our child, spouse or family member does not receive any reconciliation, as we, the guilty person, claim the center of attention, hence all of the available energy.

Often our guilt succeeds in protecting us from dealing with the feelings of the person we feel we have harmed, our child, spouse, or family member, but at the high cost of denying their feelings. And if the person who is hurt cares for us, our guilt invites, and in some cases demands that they take care of us. After all, we are the one moaning over our feeling of guilt.

We need to trust the guidance of our Higher Parent to accept responsibility for our actions without guilt, to own what we do without feeling that to do this invites punishment and pain.

Learning Detachment

Detachment is a realization that we cannot control others nor do we have to be controlled by others. Learning detachment is one of the great secrets of having a happy life. This is the Zen of living. We see. We understand. We feel, but we do not need to react and, therefore, to be controlled by the event. This basic concept is the foundation of many self-help programs, such as Al-Anon and Adult Children of Alcoholics.

We are often so quick to react and condemn that we do not take the time to see others' acts for what they are, a manifestation of themselves, and not as a comment on ourselves. To achieve detachment in some ways means not to see ourselves as so important and central to the events which surround us.

Others' thoughtless acts do not have to hurt us. But often we love the one whose barb we feel. Often we will react, and with those we love the most, our children, spouse or parents, we are prone to over-react. This rescues those we over-react with, for they must now take care of us, rather than try to understand why they upset and hurt us.

So in judging others, we rescue others. And in rescuing others by over-reacting, we deny their taking responsibility for their acts. We also deny ourselves the power we have to protect ourselves by handing over this power to another to hurt us.

How freeing it would be to let the barbs of our children and spouse elicit from us the statement, "Oh, you *are* having a bad day", rather than reducing us to tears. Then we could allow others to begin questioning their own motivation, instead of us supplying it for them.

Acknowledging Our Past

To learn detachment, we need to understand what we are detaching from; we need to acknowledge our past. In acknowledging our past we validate what our inner child knows to be true. We need to acknowledge how we were hurt, and how we still may be angry. But to do this means to make it neither more nor less than it was. Embellishing our past with more pain does not make us more worthy, it merely diminishes us in our own eyes for it means that we are denying how deeply we feel. Taking on more responsibility for what befell us does not help us. It merely indicates that we have a longer way to go to accept our past life.

Making It Worse Than It Was

For example, there are some of us who feel we must exaggerate how many beatings we received or how poor we were. We feel we must do this to justify how much rage and pain we feel. We feel that to have this much rage, or this much pain, must mean that things were worse than they were. So we are untrue to ourselves, and we hurt our inner child.

Making It Better Than It Was

And there are some of us who are so fearful of the harm we may have done, that we cannot bear to consider it. We go around vindicating ourselves and seeing only the good we have accomplished.

For instance, there are those of us who are sure that we have never, ever done anything negative to our children. If we feel any responsibility, we fear this means total responsibility. And so we shrink from it and as a result always blame someone else, perhaps much as our parents may have done if they blamed us for their life.

Does Not Help Anyone

There are those of us who are sure that we have done irreparable harm to everyone including our inner child. We tend to be so self-concerned that we have little love to share with anyone else, so we isolate. None of these extremes is beneficial to anyone.

Accepting How We Were Taught — Examining Our Family Traditions

We learn a lot about how to operate in the world from our family. In some ways being a child is the one experience that we share with all others. As Mark Twain says, "We haven't all had the good fortune to be ladies; we haven't all been generals, or poets, or statesmen; but when . . . discussing babies, we stand on common ground."

It is often within our family traditions that we learn about guilt and responsibility, and how to safely forgive ourselves, for we have witnessed this and experienced this firsthand.

Love In Every Family

Some of us have come from families with obvious problems, others from families where everything looked fairly normal on the outside. Some of us were parented very strictly, others inconsistently or others in a permissive way. There are many styles of learning guilt and responsibility and self-forgiveness, and they are all based on a foundation of how love was taught and expressed in your family of origin. But it is important to remember that in every family there was love. Sometimes perhaps it was so deeply buried as to be obscured, but love was present, even if it was not available. And it is through this love that our Higher Parent learned to guide our inner child.

A Way Of Being Safe . . . That No Longer Works

Each one of us picks a style of accepting guilt and responsibility and learning self-forgiveness, based on what our parents modeled for us, what they believed was safe. As we grew older, we adjusted this based on our personality. And we continue to modify it based on new experiences as the old way our inner child learned to be safe, no longer is safe.

This is the Step that allows us to look at how we learned to accept responsibility and how we learned to forgive ourselves as a child, and look to see how well this particular family tradition is or is not working.

Doing this will raise anxiety. We feel confused about not being loyal to how our families taught us to "take our punishment". This is normal. We all love our parents and want to be loved by them, even when we feel anger at them. Even when we feel we want to be different from them, our inner child will feel fear that they will reject us for being different. We need to accept our fear, so that our Higher Parent may quell it. To calm our inner child, we need to stay in touch with the love we have for ourselves and for others and allow the ever-present guidance of our Higher Parent.

Meditations On Parenting Your Inner Child

Know that by loving yourself in the moment, you can make amends to your inner child. Allow your great love to heal your inner child. Realize your love as your greatest healer.

Practice making amends to your inner child by forgiving yourself. Do this by cultivating an inner desire to be willing to change. Accept that in being willing to change, the ghosts of actions past will emerge. Accept these actions and their accompanying thoughts and feelings. Practice self-forgiveness by knowing that you can accept responsibility without guilt. Allow that you are not defined merely by your actions — that to act is to learn. Accept that you can separate yourself from your past with love and compassion for your inner child and with the guidance of your Higher Parent.

Know that you can actively make amends to your inner child by protecting her from the barbs of others. Love your inner child by detaching from the barbs of another, thereby not allowing these to harm you. Free your inner child's energy of the burden of judging another. Allow your inner child's energies to see, to feel and to understand.

Accept all of who you are. Free yourself of judgments of your actions. Forgive yourself for those actions which were made in error. Free yourself to learn from these actions and to go on with your life with peace and love in your heart.

Daily Self-Parenting Affirmations

I forgive and release myself to be a happy and strong person.

I release myself to live a peaceful, productive, fulfilled life.

I release those who have harmed me to go on with their lives and to do well.

I will practice loving myself by acknowledging all of my feelings.

I free myself to be in the moment, this precious moment, full of love, peace and wisdom.

CHAPTER 9

Transforming
The Promises

A.A. Step 9: Made direct amends to such people wherever possible, except when to do so would injure them or others.

Self-Parenting Step 9: Healed our inner child by realizing the promises of self-parenting in our daily living.

Hope For The Flowers

Yellow, a very special caterpillar, searches for more in life. She knows the pain of the climb. She knows that this is not for her. She knows the pain of the end of a relationship, but she will not let the pull of Stripe, her partner, make her do something that she knows is wrong for her. Still she does not know what is right for her. She trusts in herself that there must be something more in life. She wanders. And she meets a grey caterpillar spinning a cocoon. Thinking that he must be in trouble to be doing something so peculiar, she offers to help him. He signals that he is doing what he needs to do to be a butterfly. Yellow is excited. And when she asks what is a butterfly, she is told that this, a butterfly, is what she truly is. Puzzled, she questions how such a transformation is possible.

"How can I believe there's a butterfly inside . . . when all I see is a fuzzy worm?"

"You must want to fly so much that you are willing to give up being a caterpillar."

"You mean to die?"

". . . What's really you will still live. Life is changed, not taken away."

*Excerpted from **Hope for the Flowers** by Trina Paulus*

The Promises Of Health Through Self-Parenting

The struggle for so many of us is how to free and heal our inner child, for by doing this we make amends. To make amends we must leave behind many of our "old ways" and embrace the "new ways", the inner strengths, known by our Higher Parent — wisdoms which we have been gathering in these Twelve Steps.

By healthy self-parenting we can promise to use the guidance of our Higher Parent, our inner source of wisdom, to free our inner child to create a new arena, a new space where we can build bridges gently and safely, centered from our insides to the outside world. Freeing our inner child is the beginning of self-definition, self-ownership of who we are supposed to be, of who we can be.

These new abilities that we give ourselves can create an environment of self-trust which leads to increasing our self-esteem to realize our potential.

Allowing these new abilities to come to the surface takes incredible courage. Courage of the kind witnessed in the story above, where Yellow realizes that change does not mean to lose, but to have all that is possible.

1. ABUNDANCE — The Realization Of Our Needs Being Met

By defining ourselves instead of having others define us, we create abundance in our lives. We own the abundance that life has to offer if only we will accept it. By being receptive to what life has to offer us, we can own our power and be directed from within. We are no longer dependent on others, we are no longer compulsively dependent.

We realize that we are no longer limited by what we see, and that as we proceed in life each mountain climbed offers a new vista of what is possible.

We now realize that we have abundance in our relationships. We no longer isolate, no longer withdraw; we allow our inner child to connect with others.

2. SPONTANEITY — Allowing Intimacy In Our Lives

Spontaneity is the gateway through which we free our inner child so we may learn more about ourselves and the world. One way to open the gateway is to give our inner child permission to play. This means that we will free ourselves to be spontaneous. We trust the impulses of our inner child by exploring the world of play and fun, knowing that he will be protected by our Higher Parent. We can explore quietly at first, or we can just let it go and take the step to be spontaneous. The important thing to remember is that our inner child has a perspective, a unique slant on life, on the life that we need.

Not Recklessness

Being spontaneous does not mean being reckless, and potentially hurting our inner child. Such thoughts and actions are part of the old system of distrust. Acting them out will be a way of proving that the old system is right, that your inner child when left to his own devices can't be trusted, and that your impulses must be contained, restricted and subject to suspicion. Being reckless is also a way of actively hurting your inner child by staying stuck and not learning new ways, new responses.

Play

Play takes energy. When we free our energy, then we can truly be spontaneous. But freeing our energy is no easy task. To do this we must first look to see where our energy is going. One major energy block is "mind-racing" as we saw in Step 4. Other major blocks include fear of the unknown.

So how do we deal with our fear? How do babies learn? We all learned by taking small steps, falling down, laughing at ourselves and sometimes asking for help and by getting up again. We all learned in an environment made safe by a parent; we now need to make our present environment safe by using our Higher Parent.

Requires Trust

How do we free ourselves to be spontaneous? First, we begin by having our Higher Parent make it safe for spontaneity to occur. Our Higher Parent will check the limits of the impulses and make sure the environment is safe. Next we need to have our Higher Parent give our inner child permission to be spontaneous and to play. It is simple and direct. Spontaneity just requires that we trust ourselves.

To Have Intimacy

Intimacy is the sharing of our spontaneous free child with another. The degree of intimacy that we allow ourselves is the degree to which we allow ourselves to know and to accept who we are.

Intimacy is gradual. It is certainly not black or white, all or nothing. It requires time, maturity and most of all inner direction and patience. It involves taking a risk, but a risk in which we are guided by the wisdom of our Higher Parent, who allows us to choose trustworthy people in safe environments.

3. THE RESTORATION OF MANAGEABILITY IN OUR LIVES

This means no longer trying to control. By using control as our major defense, we tie up all our energy into a knot. As we saw in Step 1, trying to control produces a feeling of unmanageability in our lives. Restoring manageability into our lives means that we attempt to influence, but never to control.

Perhaps the greatest lesson of all in this is parenting. For those of us who are parents we have seen that attempting to influence our children is the only sane way of trying to raise a child. When we try to control our child, we invite him to feel resentment and to feel like a failure.

By using our power we can influence our world. This means sharing an opinion, positioning ourselves, attempting to maneuver another, but never having the ego to think we can control another. Using our influence is a great way of protecting our inner child from taking on more than his share of responsibility, and as a result, making him feel life is unmanageable.

4. LIVING IN THE PRESENT — Develop Light Side Defenses

As we saw in Step 4 our inner child needs to be protected. We can protect ourselves utilizing our dark side and as a result, have all of our defenses draining our energies, retaining compulsive self-reliance, our perfectionism and our helplessness.

Or we can learn to develop defenses from our light side, which carry us, which are protecting, freeing, nourishing. In developing lighter defenses we learn to leave the struggle behind, for we are no longer defined by what does not work.

We become more present tense focused for we realize that this is all that we need to concern ourselves with, for all that we have is the moment. This thought is freeing and keeps us balanced against just living in the past and worrying about the future.

5. SELF-DEFINITION — No Longer A Victim, Life Is No Longer A Crisis

We do not have to load the actions of others with so much of our energy, so much of our time, that they become more important than they are. We learn to ask how important is this? We learn to fit things into a framework that makes sense in our lives. A framework where we do not give others the power over us to victimize us, for we no longer define ourselves as a victim. And once we do this, life is no longer a series of crises to be survived.

We replace being a victim with an identity in which we are entitled to be angry, fearful, in a rage, but never anyone's or our own victim. We do this by owning our power to heal ourselves.

6. NEW LEGACIES: CREATING NEW TRADITIONS — Learning To Risk And To Make Choices

Learning new responses is a risky business. It means doing things in ways that may not work out perfectly the first time. It means recognizing that we have choices. It means knowing that feelings of anxiety will occur, for life is no longer only black or white. We learn to welcome anxiety, to turn it into excitement, as a sign of good orderly direction and change. And we learn that we are in charge of change and that our Higher Parent and our Higher Power will guide us through any new choice we make.

7. UNCONDITIONAL
SELF-LOVE — Self-Acceptance

By being spontaneous we learn to feel. When we free ourselves to feel, then we free ourselves to love. To be is to love. Loving ourselves is based on accepting ourselves — our imperfections, our past and, yes, our power and our future. Loving ourselves unconditionally means making a commitment to no longer hurt ourselves, no longer beat up on ourselves. Loving means trusting ourselves to be spontaneous, and trusting ourselves in this world and the next.

8. OWNING OUR SPIRITUAL SIDE — Owning
Our Totality

We realize what our true spiritual path is. We do this not by denying our intellectual side, but by reconciling it to our spiritual nature. Life is no longer a battle between intellect and spirit, but a combination of both. There is a flow between our many parts. We exist as a spring-fed lake, constantly being nourished from many sources — our many parts, our friends and family. We exist contented, at peace.

9. LEARNING TO MAKE AMENDS TO OTHERS —
Learning To Be More Than Our Acts

Having learned that we can be spontaneous, we can now begin using our new freedom. We can begin this by realizing that we are bigger than our acts. We also learn that we can be more than a one-time statement or action. We have learned that we define ourselves from our inside, from our free child, the center of goodness within us, and not from our fear or pain.

By Resolving Differences

We can implement this when we realize that we have erred and we have hurt another. We learn to free ourselves by being the first to make the overture to say, "I'm sorry," and mean it, when we are aware that we have hurt another. Saying, "I'm sorry," and meaning it, can get this issue out of the way, so we do not have to have an endless internal dialogue where our "mind races".

In taking a definitive step towards resolving whatever the problem is by admitting our part in it, we can begin to free ourselves from the re-runs of what we didn't say, or do as well as we would like. We can know that we tried our best. Remember, we are never perfect nor do we have to be. Being awkward is part of being alive.

Directly

We give ourselves plenty of practice in this on an ongoing basis, saying we are sorry when we have erred and meaning it.

We also allow ourselves to think of our past, to remember who we have hurt and to be creative in how we can let this person know that we are sorry. To do this will require using much of the growth we have gained. Sometimes this will mean that we will tell another that we are sorry. Or we may take other direct actions, such as repaying a debt. At other times it may mean that we will act so differently with them, they will know we have changed.

Indirectly

Sometimes the ability to make direct amends is difficult, for the person we would like to make amends to has died or will have no further contact with us. Or perhaps we do not know where they are. This will require us to make amends in more indirect ways, such as by making a commitment to do things differently or by being a good example to others.

We also realize that for some whom we have hurt, making true amends is not a one-time event. That to make amends means to change how we live and how we treat them and others on an ongoing basis.

10. LEARNING FORGIVENESS — Learning To See Others In Totality

The other side of making amends to others is to forgive them. We no longer punish them, we no longer blame them. We release them and as a result we release ourselves.

By forgiving others we lighten our burden of anger and fear. To forgive others means that we accept what they have done. We feel our reactions to what they have done. We attempt to understand what they have done. *And We Let It Go.*

11. MAKING AMENDS TO OUR INNER CHILD — Learning Self-Forgiveness

This is a major step for each of us to take — to learn to make amends to our inner child. We need to learn to forgive ourselves for when we didn't protect ourselves as we should have done. We need to stop our "inner war" of having a racing mind and punishing thoughts.

We learned about self-forgiveness in Step 8. Here in Step 9 is where we begin to implement self-forgiveness. We make amends to ourselves by no longer beating ourselves up for what we did or thought that we now regret. We accept our imperfections. In fact we may even learn to smile or laugh at our imperfections, those parts of us that make us unique. We make amends to our inner child by:

Our Commitment To Change

By risking living our life differently we can begin to make amends to our inner child. We now know that we can live differently. We now know that there is another way. We make amends by our courage to change.

Our Willingness To Laugh

We free our inner child to feel when we have the courage to laugh at what life brings us. We free our inner child when we allow ourselves to feel our pain, our love, our disappointment, knowing that there is a release at the end of each of these feelings and in this release is the joy of our inner child.

Our Great Love For Who We Are — How We Value Ourselves

In our acceptance of who we are comes the love for all that we are, our unconditional self-love. Our inner child and our Higher Parent produce our uniqueness, which the outside world may sometimes see as imperfections. Our feelings, which some may feel threatened by and try to dismiss as sentimentality or fierceness, and our true power, our real self, are the core of our strength.

Our Willingness To Live In The Present

By living in the present we revel in what is ours to enjoy. No longer are we controlled by the past. No longer are we anxious about the future. We now are centered by our love and are in full possession of the moment, knowing that by being in the moment, the past is no longer of any consequence, and the future will be taken care of itself.

Our Desire For Intimacy, To No Longer Live Alone

We are now able to risk being with others safely and can allow ourselves to be seen and touched by another. We no longer need to isolate, we no longer mistrust others. We are no longer addicted to empty wells. By understanding how to trust ourselves more completely, we now allow trustworthy people into our life. We are now full wells and *we attract other full wells to share in our life.*

12. MOVING ON WITH LIFE — Leaving Childhood Trauma Behind And Growing

It takes courage to leave the struggle behind. It takes freedom to live in the present. It takes trust to look forward to the future. To move on with our lives, we need to learn to leave the struggle behind by risking doing things differently. This means allowing our Higher Parent to guide us in learning new ways. To do this we need to have our Higher Parent give our inner child permission to experiment.

We can keep our inner child from experimenting by holding him tight, shutting his eyes, keeping him still, telling him the world is a terrible, wicked place and he must be protected and taught to stay afraid.

Or we can free our inner child by using our Higher Parent. Our inner child will know how to get his needs met for he can trust his inner guidance, the voice of our Higher Parent and Higher Power as it speaks to our inner child.

Instead of defining ourselves by what does not work, by what we are afraid of, we can define ourselve by what we see as possible. By doing this, we leave the struggle behind and create new possibilities and new legacies.

Leaving Shame Behind

Shame creates a negative feeling, it keeps us stuck in the past. Sorrow for what we have done creates corrective action leading to forgiveness of ourselves and others. When we take responsibility for our negative acts and feel our sorrow, we can learn to repent, to forgive and to transform ourselves. True sorrow for the past leads to resolution. It creates the opportunity for new beginnings, and allows us to leave past traumas behind.

Shame and guilt lead to the "beating ourselves up" devaluation of ourselves as "bad". Shame and guilt are often taught in many dysfunctional families. In fact they are characteristics that can make a family dysfunctional.

Leaving The Struggle Behind

Moving on with our life means recognizing the many negative family traditions that we have been taught and freeing ourselves to write new traditions. It means leaving the tradition of shame and humiliation behind, as well as the other traditions learned in childhood which devalue us. It means learning to take responsibility for ourselves without guilt.

Becoming The Free Child We Were Meant To Be

We see, we feel, we accept, and we move beyond. We do not content ourselves in staying fixed in an empty well. We become full wells, and we attract full wells in our life. We join with others to support us and to love us. We are no longer the victim, but are transformed by our power and inner wisdom, into a free child full of intuitive wisdom.

Meditations On Parenting Your Inner Child

Embrace your spontaneous inner child. Practice forgiving yourselves and know that you can make amends to your inner child. Know that what you learn to do for yourselves, you can do with others. Let this be just one manifestation that you have of your love. Transform yourselves with the love you have for your inner child. Allow this love to shine through you and within you to guide and protect you. Believe in the promises of healthy self-parenting. Know that you have the power and love to realize these in your life.

Know that you have the power to see choices and to make them. Own the power you have to see what is available for you in this world. By making a conscious choice, know that you can begin to move aside your conscious choices. Allow yourselves to own that what you want is to leave the struggle behind.

Follow your spiritual path. Practice not being alone by allowing the God within you to nourish you. Practice loving your Higher Power by acting in accordance with the wishes of the God presence you worship.

Daily Self-Parenting Affirmations

I free myself to see choices and to act on those opportunities that are best for me.

I free myself to be spontaneous and to follow my inner, my loved, child.

I free myself of my past painful memories, knowing dwelling on them keeps me in this painful place. In their place I put hope, love and options for a fulfilled future.

I free myself to live the promises of daily Self-Parenting.

CHAPTER 10

Self-Acceptance: How We Value Ourselves

> *A.A. Step 10: Continued to take personal inventory and when we were wrong promptly admitted it.*
>
> ―――――――――
>
> *Self-Parenting Step 10: Practiced daily self-acceptance and learned to live in the present.*

Good Luck? Bad Luck?

There is a Chinese story of an old farmer who had an old horse for tilling his fields. One day the horse escaped into the hills and when all the farmer's neighbors sympathized with the old man over his bad luck, the farmer replied. "Bad luck? Good luck? Who knows?"

A week later the horse returned with a herd of wild horses from the hills and this time the neighbors congratulated the farmer on his good luck. His reply again was, "Good luck? Bad luck? Who knows?"

Then when the farmer's son was attempting to tame one of the wild horses, he fell off its back and broke his leg. Everyone thought this very bad luck. Not the farmer, whose only reaction was, "Bad luck? Good luck? Who knows?"

Some weeks later the army marched into the village and conscripted every able-bodied youth they found there. When they saw the farmer's son with his broken leg, they let him off. Now was that good luck? Bad luck? Who knows?

(Doubleday, 1978)
*From **Sadhana: A Way To God**
by Anthony De Mello*

Black And White Thinking

So often when an event happens to us, we rush to understand it immediately, rather than to experience it, feel it and accept it. We use our cognitive self to categorize the experience. We ask ourselves, "Is it black or is it white?" We ponder over "Are we yet again a victim? Or have we just barely escaped?" We attempt to filter our experience through the lens of good luck or bad luck, much like the farmer's neighbors.

We do this because we are frightened. We do this because this is the only way we can control what has just occurred. We see life as black or white to protect ourselves from the pain of ambiguity, from the uncertainty of a grey world. We do this so we can immediately digest the experience and be ready for the next sling or arrow, for the next crisis.

By living our life from crisis to crisis we pay a great price. We impose reasons on events, reasons that may not be accurate, but which fit our view of ourselves in the world as needing to be compulsively self-reliant, as a victim of circumstances over which we have no control. We see ourselves as the unlucky one. We deny ourselves the guidance of our Higher Parent; we define ourselves as powerless.

Staying Stuck — Staying In Crisis

The price we pay is that we keep ourselves "stuck". Yes, we get an adrenalin charge when we face yet another crisis. Yes, we know "how to handle" the situation. Yes, we know that we are strong. So there are positives to maintaining this world view of black and white thinking for we are always ready for action, a posture we prefer.

But there are drawbacks for we continue to see the world as a place where we cannot get our needs met, as a place where we cannot be nurtured. And because we see the world this way, we continue to create a reality where this occurs. Because we need to simplify our world, we do what comes naturally, we interpret all events as negative, which maintains our family tradition of seeing the world as all good or all bad. We stay loyal to what our family has taught us, but we also stay stuck and in crisis.

Learning To Accept Events As Neutral

The way out of what has become a self-fulfilling prophecy, seeing ourselves as the "wronged one", is to learn to accept events as more neutral. We need to understand, as the farmer did, that many events in life are random. And most of all, we need to realize that the power that we bring to any event is the personal interpretation that we give it.

We Create Our Reality

In many ways we create our own reality. We do this by how we allow ourselves to respond, by how much importance we attach to any event, by how we allow ourselves personally to take what has occurred. We do this by deciding how much pressure we will place on ourselves to know what to do and to do it. We do this by our acceptance of our own feelings, by deciding to use our inner wisdom, our Higher Parent, to guide our judgment, rather than relying on our fear and negative thinking, our dark side, to interpret the world for us.

Our interpretation of life is within our control. What has worked against us, the energy we used, in seeing life as making us a victim, can now work in our favor. If we own our power, our Higher Parent self, we can use this to re-define ourselves to create a world full of self-affirmation, where events don't govern us, a world where we act and do not react.

Accepting Our Own Lack Of Perfection — No More Hiding

To do this we need to accept ourselves fully. This is the Step in which we actively create new traditions by giving ourselves permission to live in grey and to make mistakes. By doing this we accept ourselves. We give ourselves permission to experiment with different viewpoints. We learn to say to ourselves "Here I am with my assets and debts, and I can acknowledge and accept them all." No more hiding, no more pretending.

We learn to know who we are, and to accept who we are. By accepting ourselves we transfigure ourselves. We take on a new form, full of love and inner peace.

We become less reactive and more contemplative. We become more accepting. We become more patient, less in a rush to make things black or white, more willing to be awkward, stumble and trust through the grey.

We realize that we can do this because we have learned to trust ourselves. We have learned to take care of our inner child, by not putting him or her down, as we were used to doing but by releasing our self-acceptance and granting ourselves peace.

The Power Of Self-Acceptance

There is such power in self-acceptance, for to the degree that we accept who we are is the degree that we value who we are.

By being honest with ourselves we free our energies. We change our relationships with others. We model self-acceptance by such concrete actions as diffusing disputes with our spouse by willingly accepting our part, and only our part, in what went awry. We model acceptance for imperfection for our children, even if they are in college or with families of their own.

Accepting Mistakes

Our acceptance of not being perfect was the work of Step 6. It is now time to implement this permission in our daily affairs by admitting to ourselves and to others, "I made a mistake." This is the clear statement of someone who has inner peace free from inner judgments. It is the statement of someone in touch with their Higher Parent.

Our admission of our error should be the long and the short of it. In doing this we have allowed ourselves to understand that we made a mistake. We probably have done nothing unusual or anything that cannot be changed. We just slipped and did not use good judgment, or did not think something through. That is all. Nobody died. We haven't caused a worldwide famine. We just made a mistake. In doing this we are guided by our Higher Parent, to release our energy by owning the truth. There is such power in being truthful. To be truthful releases us to be in the present, free, with all of our energies unencumbered.

Is Not The End Of The World

We learn to de-catastrophize events. We no longer see events as black and white. We now see grey, dark grey at times, but rarely do we see black. We are no longer crisis oriented, but we accept that at times this part of us will re-emerge and we will catastrophize an event.

Now we know how to take off this mask for we understand the feelings beneath the mask. We accept that we will make things worse as a way of energizing ourselves to deal with an event. We learn to accept this, to anticipate when it will be more likely to occur and to not indulge this part of us that thrives on simple answers and action.

We can accept this part of ourselves for we realize that a mistake is not the end of the world, but merely a one-time event. In being able to say this to ourselves, we will be able to hear this being said by others and to accept their mistakes. We will also be able to model acceptance of others' errors, and make room for others to tell us our errors, without the fear that we will attack them out of defensive fear.

Accepting Parents

By accepting and freeing ourselves, we also begin to accept our roots, our parents. The degree to which we accept our parents is the degree to which we value them. We learn to accept, even if it still brings up pain, that our parents were not all that we wanted and needed them to be. But now we begin to see them as human and accept that they were not all that they wanted to be either. Particularly if they also lived with an alcoholic or abusive parent. We accept that they made mistakes.

Whose Love Was So Powerful

We accept that they also loved us with a love that was so powerful that we may have had to distance from it. We understand, particularly if we are parents ourselves, that a mother's or father's love can be overwhelming. That a parent can love a child even more than they love their own life. And that a child can perhaps feel responsible for a parent's feelings of love and feel obliged to take care of the parent, feel pressured to repay their love.

In families with alcoholism or similar trauma, we accept that this love was always present, even if it was not always available. This means that love may have been expressed indirectly, through actions and worry or passionately, perhaps through disagreements or symbolically through gestures and traditions. We understand that a love expressed this way can be confusing for a child, and that this confusion led us perhaps to the conclusion that we were not loved, or worse that we were not lovable.

By our acceptance and understanding of the past, of how we were loved, we begin the process of making peace with our parents and ourselves.

Wearing The World As A Loose Garment

Making a mistake does not mean that we have to like the fact that we have made a mistake or to expect that we will not have angry or disappointed feelings when someone makes a mistake that involves us. It means that we will realize that it is only a mistake, and not see it as part of "only bad things happen to us" or "someone has it in for us". These viewpoints make us much too important, and much more the center of what happens around us than can ever be true. In this way we become less intense and easier to be around.

In learning to accept that we and others make mistakes, we can 'let it go' and not embellish the mistake with reasons and explanations that dig us and others into a hole. We can make room for letting things slide, not having to make a major case out of every miscalculation our spouses, loved ones or friends make. We can learn to wear the world as a loose garment, keeping things in perspective!

Letting Go Of Anger And Disappointment

Accepting mistakes for what they are, frees us. In some cases this may mean looking back on past events in your life and realizing that your parents or spouse, friend or child were guilty of making a mistake and not of intentionally trying to harm you.

With this realization that we all make mistakes, comes the opportunity to act as a healthy role model for our children, even if they are no longer at home, for our spouse, and maybe even our parents. We learn that we can accept their missteps, mistakes, in life — and to do this all with love. No longer will mistakes need to be considered as reasons to be punished and not to be loved.

The result of this process is to free the energy surrounding our inner child to again experience the joy that is present in every moment.

The Price We Pay By Hiding

When as a child we learned that we could not make mistakes, we learned to hide and pretend and most of all we learned that we can never be good enough. We learned not to accept and value ourselves. We often unwittingly continued this tradition with our own children, with our co-workers and in our most intimate relationships. We hide, we adapt to what others need, we lose who we are.

Even today when we do not accept our mistakes, we begin to fill up with the "garbage" of the past again. Not accepting our mistakes is not accepting who we are and is a sign that we are slipping back into the old ways, perfectionism and self-criticism. When we hide who we are from ourselves, we create dishonesty and tension within.

Mistakes — An Opportunity To Grow

Mistakes can now be seen as growth opportunities. They represent the lessons in life where the old way didn't work and a new way needs to be found. Our Higher Parent can guide us through this new understanding. This new perspective is exciting and can also be a bit scary, for change has a way of inviting in the unknown. But with the planning we have done in the previous steps, change can now be implemented, based on what we have learned about ourselves, and what we have gleaned from our real-life experiences. Certainly if we all learned from our mistakes, instead of repeating them, this would be a very different and more fulfilled life.

Taking A Daily Inventory

Learning from mistakes and living in the present is accomplished by taking a daily inventory. In this way there can be no backlog of guilt or of anger. Here, guided by our Higher Parent, when we are wrong we admit to it, and see how we can resolve the issue another way. By admitting to our wrongs, we also short-circuit our tendency to blame ourselves, sometimes mercilessly, for what we have done.

Modeling daily self-honesty is freeing. We no longer need to hide our actions from ourselves or from those we are the closest to. We no longer need to pretend and to invalidate our own reality. We can now accept ourselves and others.

Mistakes are admitted to, this inevitably takes less energy than covering them up. Wrongs are adjusted, not punished by self-recriminations or extreme reactions, such as withdrawing, saying mean statements or lashing out. By so doing we fully accept who we are, and we begin to accept those others who inhabit our world.

Living In The Present — Living Cleanly

There is a saying, "Life is now in session, are you present?" Living in the now allows us to be present to life. When we can learn to accept our mistakes and those of our children, spouse, friends and even our own parents, then we live in the present. Steps 1 to 9 have helped us clean house, understand what has happened, what we have done and why. We have now searched the corners of our mind for memories that cried out for attention and forgiveness. We have gone back and reconciled ourselves to what was and cannot be altered. We have felt, grieved and forgiven ourselves and others. Now is the time to go forward.

Steps 10 to 12 are the present and future steps. They help us live in the present and to project new and happier traditions into the future. These are the steps that help us resolve the trauma of the past and go forward.

Living in the present is a new tradition. It is a new gift for us and for our children, our spouse and friends. It can even be a gift that we offer to our parents as a token for our forgiveness.

Living in the present is most of all a gift to our inner child. It is a way of being, exploring and spending energy savoring the moment, no longer enmeshed with the past and dreading the future.

As Isaiah is quoted in the Bible, "Remember not the former things, nor consider the things of old. Behold, I am doing a new thing" (Isaiah 43: 18-19).

Meditations On Parenting Your Inner Child

Embrace the truth. Know that from the truth you will derive your energy and hope. Know that to be truthful releases you to be in the present, free with all of your energies available. Know that in the truth lies your acceptance of your true value and the true value of others.

Give yourself the joy of living in the present. Allow the mistakes that you and others have made to be the work of the past — there like the color of the wall, but no longer having any emotional intensity about them.

Give yourself the gift of wearing the world as a loose garment. Allow yourself the gift of perspective. Give yourself the gift of time to decide how you will act in any situation. Know that all events are neutral, that you create your own reality by how you choose to interpret the events around you. Allow your Higher Parent to guide you.

Daily Self-Parenting Affirmations

I live in the present, knowing that in this realm I will experience love and peace.

I acknowledge my errors, along with my strengths, knowing that in self-acceptance lies my true value.

I experience life around me, rather than rushing to understand it or judge it.

I transfigure myself into a being full of love and self-acceptance for all that I have done and all that I will do.

I forgive myself and others all errors without punishment, for in punishing, I only drain myself of energy.

I free myself to be me, and accept myself with all of my imperfections. In doing this I am also open to accepting my children, spouse and parents, and freeing them to love me and receive my love.

CHAPTER 11

Living In The Light

A.A. Step 11: Sought through prayer and meditation to improve our conscious contact with God as we understood Him, *praying only for knowledge of His will for us and the power to carry that out.*

Self-Parenting Step 11: We allowed the divinity in us to shine forth by surrendering to our Higher Power.

We are not human beings sharing our spiritual experience.
We are spiritual beings sharing our human experience.

Anonymous

"Oh, Great Spirit, teach me to think quietly, to speak gently
and to hear thy voice in the whispering breeze, the songs of the
birds and in the murmuring brook."

Old Cherokee Prayer

Practicing The Daily Presence Of God

Children's concept of God is very simple. God to children is a benevolent older friend or a loving forgiving parent. God to children is a being to whom they have full access. God is a force for good that will work personally on their behalf, even without their asking for this help. God is their protector. God is a being who totally knows them and understands them and accepts them, and most of all unconditionally loves them.

Children know how to be in the presence of their Higher Power. If you talk to little children about their relationship to God, you will find that they talk to God often and even play games with God. They know how to practice the presence of God in their daily life, something we often forget to do by the time we become adults. That is why scripture talks of us needing to be as little children in our faith. When we approach our spirituality as a child, we learn to forgive ourselves as we instinctively know that God forgives us. When we approach God as a child, we approach God with no expectations.

Our Higher Parent And God

Our Higher Parent is the seat of our intuitive knowledge. Intuitive knowledge is knowledge that is from a deeper place within us than our reason. As adults we have learned to rely on our reason to guide us, thinking that there would always be a logical answer to everything. Many of us have become creatures of logic sacrificing our feelings and intuitive knowledge on the altar of logic.

Logic can only take us so far, then it becomes useless. The wonder of the stars, the ecstasy of love, the birth of a child are not appreciated through logic. They are appreciated through our capacity for awe and understood through our transcendental self, our Higher Parent.

Our Higher Parent is our direct channel to our Higher Power. Our Higher Parent is the seat of our inner wisdom which flows from the divinity within us. It is our beacon which can guide us through the storms and dark times. It will sort out the chaff from the wheat and lead us, if we let it, to centered spiritual lives.

Meditation — A Road To Recovery

Westerners have a problem understanding the process of meditation. For most westerners the process may seem too passive. Spiritual listening skills are underdeveloped in western society, where technological achievements are more valued than spiritual insight. That is why we have accomplished so much as a society but still feel empty on a personal level.

Anne Wilson Schaef says that we have become an addicted society seeking fulfillment from the outside in, rather than the inside out. We are so busy focusing on action that we have forgotten the art of contemplation. We have come to value the world around us and ignore the world within. Meditation is the way to reconnect to our deeper values. It is a way for us to be inner directed in an outer directed world.

Meditation is the best way to access our Higher Parent's wisdom on a daily basis. Meditation is a way of stilling the mind so a higher level of consciousness can emerge. Meditation is a conscious stilling of self. It is the launching pad for transcending our ego and connecting with God.

Meditation is the way we take corrective action on an inner level and change attitudes and beliefs. Meditation is the process by which we free our inner child from the bondage of hate and fear and liberate his energies to use for greater fulfillment as an adult.

There are many ways to meditate. One method for meditation was explained in Step 4 through the process of *stop thinking*. There are meditations which are based on chanting sounds and meditations which are based on visualizations. There are meditations which are based on the contemplation of spiritual laws and meditations based on the saying of ritual prayers.

Eastern literature is full of information on how to meditate. Your local house of worship, ashram or community college will have classes on meditation. If you look around, you will find the guidance you need. The important point is to get started and make a habit of looking within yourself for answers. The important point is to create regular opportunities for you to learn from your Higher Parent.

Prayer

Prayer is different from meditation. Prayer is an offering up. Prayer is being in love with God, while meditation is paying attention to what God has to say to you through your Higher Parent.

There are many forms of prayer. There is, for instance, learned and spontaneous prayer. As Father Catior says in his book *You Are The Light Of The World,* "Unlearned or spontaneous prayer is prayer that wells up in the heart, the prayer God teaches you Himself. Learned prayer is what you pick up from your tradition. Certain prayers are learned or memorized.

"Each of us comes from a culture that teaches us the proper and acceptable way to approach God. There is clerical prayer, rabbinical prayer, imam and shaman prayer. Such prayers are learned through training and practice. But unlearned prayer comes from the depths of the soul."

Just as in meditation it does not matter what form of prayer you use as long as you pray daily, expressing your devotion to your Higher Power, asking for guidance and listening for the answers. What is important is your intention to do God's will in your life and to seek out God as a loving light to guide your life.

Living As An Act Of Prayer

All of us make mistakes even when we are trying to do the right thing. We can't think of all the possible outcomes of all our acts. But we can be clear on the intention of our acts. We can look into our hearts and see whether we are acting out of jealousy, spite, greed or love. In searching our hearts for the truth, we find how close or far away from our inner child we are. In seeking to have right intention, we free our inner child to lead us in the direction of love. When we have clear intention to do God's will, we are living in the light, even when our intentions don't work out.

Right Intention — Doing God's Will

Most of us get more caught up in defining our spiritual beliefs than practicing them in our lives. A true spiritual life is determined by the way we live, not by what we say.

When we live with the consciousness of God in our lives, when we allow the healing energies of love to imbue our lives with direction from a greater source, we make our living an act of prayer, we become an example of the spirit working through us.

Living a spiritual life means having God as a background thought. It means maintaining contact with your Higher Parent and your Higher Power. It means judging your actions through the filter of God's will. It means living each day in a spirit of gratitude. It means looking for the spark of divine light in everyone you meet regardless of the circumstance. It means to pray without ceasing with the absolute faith that all your prayers will be answered in an abundant universe.

Allowing The Divinity Within

We have been taught to seek freedom through individualism. In our rush to seek out for ourselves all that life has to offer we have lost sight of the greatest gift of all . . . each other. Instead of finding freedom, we are imprisoned by our own self-interest; as Mother Marie des Douleurs said in her book, *Joy Out Of Sorrow,* "The obstinacy of a mind obsessed with itself forges a thousand chains from which it is impossible to free oneself."

When we practice prayer and meditation on a daily basis, when we surrender ourselves to our Higher Parent's guidance, we free ourselves from our chains and allow the divinity within to shine through. When we create the bridge to our Higher Power so that we may do this, we learn to live in the light.

From this place real inner healing will take place. From this place real forgiveness will be available for yourself and others. From this place you can truly leave behind the pain and trauma of childhood and liberate yourself from your past.

From this place you will be able to find real freedom and joy by letting go of bitterness and mistrust and living in the fullness of your loving energies. You will be able to create new relationships with your parents and loved ones based on understanding and forgiveness. You will be able to create true intimacy in your lives and never be alone again.

From this place you will be able to find a greater understanding. An understanding that comes from a daily connection to your Higher Parent, your Higher Power and the cosmos.

Meditations On Parenting Your Inner Child

Acknowledge the source of inner wisdom within you, your Higher Parent. Invite your Higher Parent to lead you to listen for answers. Visualize yourself bathed in light. Visualize your Higher Parent holding your inner child in his arms. Accept this as the true reality of your life. Let your Higher Parent nurture your inner child.

Practice letting go of your reliance on logic. Center yourself in a quiet place; allow your mind to be stilled. Follow your breath, concentrating only on the flow in and out of your breathing. When your mind is stilled, ask a question that you need an answer to. Allow your intuitive intelligence to emerge from your Higher Parent. Surrender your will to this intuitive side.

Pray from your heart. Visualize yourself talking to God as though he were your best friend. Share all your feelings with God, your joy and pain, your anger and compassion, asking for the knowledge of God's will in your life and the power to carry that out. Let yourself feel the spiritual energy released within you when you pray with your heart.

Daily Self-Parenting Affirmations

Each day I use the endless wisdom available to me in the form of my Higher Parent, to draw closer to my Higher Power and God's plan for me.

As a child of the light I have endless resources and energy for doing good in the world.

As just one of the Creator's children each day I grow in love and respect for all living things and elements on Mother Earth.

Just as God forgives me, I forgive my parents and all other people who have hurt me and invite them into my heart; my heart is full of forgiveness.

CHAPTER 12

Reaching Out:
Learning To Give What We
Have Received

A.A. Step 12: Having had a spiritual awakening as the result of these steps, we tried to carry this message to other alcoholics, and to practice these principles in all our affairs.

Self-Parenting Step 12: Having had this spiritual awakening, we reached out to others in the spirit of giving, love and community.

Loving Our Spirit — Our Inner Child

The Spirit comprehends himself
In the power of will
Alone, free
Ever-creating,
All irradiating . . .
Divinely playing
In the multiplicity of forms.

He comprehends himself
In the thrill of life
In the desire for blossoming,
In the love-struggle.
The Spirit playing,
The Spirit flitting,
With eternal aspiration
Creating ecstasy,
Surrenders to the bliss of love.
Amid the flowers of his creation
He lingers in freedom.

The Spirit is at the height of being.
And he feels
The tide unending
Of the divine power,
Of free will.
He is all-daring
What menaced —
Now is excitement,
What terrified
Is now delight;
And the bites of panthers and
hyenas
have become
But a new caress,
A new pang,
And the sting of the serpent
But a burning kiss.
And the universe resounded
With a joyful cry,
"I am."

*from **Poem of Ecstasy** by Alexander Scriabin*

Being The Teacher And The Student —
Reaching Out With Love

Having achieved this state of inner love and peace through our work within each of these steps, our energy can now be inspired. We can cry, *"I Am,"* knowing the full meaning of this simple truth. In this new sober, reflective and sometimes joyous mood, we can become ready for a new action — teaching others.

And what will we teach others? We will teach of our journey, of how we were filled with pain and the memories that haunted us until we found the guidance of our God and our Higher Parent and the unconditional love of our inner child. As a result, we found an inner direction. We will teach our process, our steps. And we will teach our transfiguration, the changes wrought within us and through us.

Teaching others gives us even more riches than we can imagine. By teaching others we gain. Every question, each skeptical remark represents a new gift for it allows us to yet again go over the ground that we know so well from another angle, another perspective.

Our constantly changing prism of knowledge sheds new lights with each subtle change in angle, and brings us closer to the knowledge of our inner child and of our Higher Power.

You Cannot Keep It Unless You Give It Away

By giving now we can receive. By sharing the knowledge of our Higher Parent and the joy of our inner child with others, we also delve deeper into this knowledge ourselves. Remember, we cannot share what we do not have.

By sharing we can own what we know. We may at times be surprised by what we say, or even more surprised by what we do. As we grow, we may be even more surprised by how old reactions, such as being quick to defend ourselves or depend on others for approval instead of trusting ourselves, are no longer how we choose to be in the world.

By sharing we are forced to recognize the changes within us. By sharing we strengthen our commitment to loving our inner child.

Carrying The Message — Learning How To Teach Others

There are as many ways to teach as there are ways to be.

The most important way is to be an example of the program in all our affairs. Some of us may have special roles such as a teacher. This will involve actually standing in front of a group of young or adult students. For others our additional role will allow us to work with clients in therapy and shed new lights on their difficulties.

Being a parent offers yet another opportunity of modeling our growth within our family, by using the new ways we have discovered to handle life's never-ending challenges and opportunities. It also means firing our children from the job of being *our* parents and allowing them to have what we missed, a childhood. All of us have opportunities to teach others in direct and indirect ways just by using the program in the other 23 hours of the day, the hours when we are not attending a meeting.

Recognizing The Rewards Of Our Patience — Our Spiritual Awakening

By being patient we are rewarded. We recognize that most spiritual experiences are slow, gradual, more like the unfolding of a flower than a thunderbolt. Our sharing of our spiritual side makes this clearer and more profound.

We realize that the basis of our action is the spiritual awakening we have experienced. Our spiritual awakening is the realization of God, of a Higher Power, who is active within our life. This new relationship with our spiritual side is the source of our new found strength in the world.

We are patient for we have surrendered to God's will. We do not need to be controlled by "mind-racing". We pray only that we may know God's will for us and have the strength to follow it.

We have learned to follow the inner urgings of our soul, our Higher Parent. We have learned to heed the voice of our inner child, for this is the voice that God will often choose to use to speak within us.

Leaving Crisis Behind — Dependent No More

We Have Changed Our Responses

We know now that we do not need our life changed instantly; for we have changed within. By our patience we have changed how we respond. The same cannons may go off, the same quicksand surrounds us but we have changed how we respond.

We See Options

No longer is life black or white. (We see options.) Yes, it is more complex, but we have learned to handle the anxiety which more options bring. We have learned to love ourselves within our anxiety. We have learned to accept our feelings, all of them, even those that bring in the unknown.

We Make Choices

We are no longer tied to our family traditions which dictate what choices we may see and what choices we must make. (We now make choices.) We are the free child, free to experiment, to play, to make mistakes and to learn.

We Are Motivated From Within Not Without

We are no longer crisis oriented. We do not need to be motivated by having a crisis in our life to conquer and become energized by the battle. (We have learned to internalize our motivation.) We are now motivated by what our Higher Parent sees is best for us, best for our inner child. We can plan ahead with the fuller knowledge of who we are and what we will need. Our patience in working our program is rewarded.

We No Longer Need To Relive Trauma In Order To Feel

In the past we would conjure up, or they would appear unbidden, memories, painful childhood memories of being unloved, emotionally or physically hurt, perhaps even of incest. These memories became like a scab on our soul that we would pick on, make bleed and finally in this process we could allow ourselves to feel. For many of us this was the only way we could feel; this was the only way that we could connect our emotions to an action. And so we relived each memory, and eventually succeeded in retraumatizing ourselves each time that we did.

We can now connect our feelings to what we are experiencing outside of us, as well as inside of us. We can now feel in all colors, in all dimensions. (To feel no longer means to feel only trauma.) We are now entitled to all of our feelings. We now can feel all of our feelings.

We do not have to fear punishment, for we realize that we can validate our own feelings. We do not need to fear losing control, for we know that we are in charge of how we choose to act.

We Learn To Move On With Our Life

Our transfiguration is the resolution of our pain. Here we have gone beyond our experiences and extracted a new meaning, a new purpose. We are no longer defined by what happened to us as children; we are transfigured by these experiences. We realize that these experiences, as painful as they are, are not an ending point, but a beginning. They form a point of departure for us to define who we are by what we will do with what we are given.

And it is through moving on with our lives, that we embrace our true spiritual path. For as we leave behind the empty wells, we make ready to become full wells. As we learn to attract full wells to us in our life, we can teach others by our example to do the same.

We have then redefined our life by not limiting ourselves by what happened to us. (We define our life by the choices we have created.)

Finally we model for our own children the spirit of community and social responsibility that was lacking in our own childhoods.

Giving To Our Community — Practicing The Principles

True health is judged not just by how we live our personal lives, but how we contribute to the world we live in. It is not enough to work to find personal fulfillment and ignore the greater community of humankind. Each of us must find a purpose in life greater than our own self-interest or we recreate the cycle of self-centeredness that we have worked so hard to break.

This was the wisdom of the founders of Alcoholics Anonymous, who saw that only by reaching out to others could recovering alcoholics maintain sobriety and learn the lesson of self-sacrifice. As those of us in OA, AA, NA, ACoA, Al-Anon and others in the self-help movement know, one candle in the night can dispel the darkness.

One candle in the night can warm the frozen heart. We have experienced our own hearts opening up touched by the light, just as we have touched others with our own light. There are still children lost in the cycle of alcoholism, drug addiction and child abuse. They still fall asleep alone at night as we did, confused and hurt and feeling responsible for the pain and hurt in their families. They have closed their hearts to the light. They need us.

Each of us can light the night as children of the light! We live in a world still caught in great darkness and suffering. Even as many of us in the self-help movement recover from the effects of addiction, even more of our brothers and sisters still live in ignorance and fear. They need us.

As Martin Luther King, Jr., said, "If we do not find for ourselves something worth dying for, we have nothing worth living for."

The need is great and we are few but powerful in our love and spirituality. We are the hope for the future. As we join together in God's plan for a new age of love, fellowship and joy, each of us must find that cause beyond ourselves which binds us to the greater community or our recovery will be incomplete and hollow.

Each of us must find that cause worth dying for if our life is to have real value! We live in an addicted society, lost, seeking to find itself in things outside itself. As survivors we have a responsibility to carry the message, to share the good news that fear is an illusion and finally, that abundance and love are the real legacies of humankind.

Meditations On Parenting Your Inner Child

Embrace your spiritual awakening. Visualize yourself as a flower opening up in the warmth of a rising sun. Let the sun warm you, feel the sun traveling down your stem to your roots deep in the ground. Feel yourself opening up in the light of the sun. Experience this opening up as a spiritual awakening. Allow yourself to fully realize the new path, the spiritual path that you have embarked upon.

Allow yourself to relish in your choices, your options. Allow your inner child to delight in this new world filled with so many things. Allow the voice of your Higher Parent to be clear crystal vibrating within you and guiding you. Accept that you are now inner directed, that you define what happens to you, that you are no longer defined from without, but defined from within. Feel the feelings that come up as this is entertained, as this is embraced. This is the real truth about who you are. Realize that your transfiguration is the resolution of your pain. Welcome your inner process and keep with your inner journey, your inner path. *Accept that you cannot fail.*

Recognize the fact that we are all connected to one another and responsible for one another and for Mother Earth. Imagine yourself in your home, then imagine yourself flying over your home. Next imagine yourself over the town or city where you live and as you now fly higher, imagine you can see the region where you live. As you fly higher still, you can see the outline of your country.

Finally as you leave the Earth's atmosphere, you can see Mother Earth spinning in space, just one of the Creator's many planets in a wondrous cosmos full of planets and suns. Let yourself feel the delicacy of Mother Earth. Open your heart to her and commit yourself to feeling your love for her.

Feel your gratitude to the Creator for all the gifts you have been given. And as you descend back to Mother Earth, allow yourself to feel your kinship with all living things and the elements and commit yourself to do one thing each day to help someone else and not tell anyone about it. Commit yourself to show your love to one child still lost in the chaos of addiction and abuse. Commit yourself and know that God's Will will be done through you.

Daily Self-Parenting Affirmations

I welcome my spiritual path, knowing that it will lead me where I need to go.

I allow myself choices and in doing so, free myself from the yoke of those family traditions that bound me to my painful past.

I give myself inner direction and inner validation, knowing that these allow me and not my past to dictate my future.

I TRANSFIGURE myself into a whole human being, knowing that my past is but one part of me, knowing that I can control how I choose to respond. Trusting in my Higher Parent within and God to guide me and strengthen me for the future, I am transformed.

I acknowledge my responsibility to my brothers and sisters in the animal, plant and mineral kingdoms and grow in love for all the inhabitants of Mother Earth day by day.

Professional Care.
Professional Concern.
Professional Counselor . . .
just for you!

Brought to you by Health Communications, Inc., *Professional Counselor* is dedicated to serving the addictions and mental health fields. With Richard Fields, Ph.D., an authority in Dual Diagnosis, serving as editor, and in-depth articles and columns written by and for professionals, you will get the timely information you need to best serve your clients. *Professional Counselor*'s coverage includes:

- Treatment advances
- Mental health and addictions research
- Family, group and special populations therapy
- The latest in counseling techniques
- Listing of upcoming workshops and events
- Managed care and employee assistance programs

Professional Counselor: Serving the Addictions and Mental Health Fields is <u>the</u> magazine for counselors, therapists, addictionologists, psychologists, managed-care specialists and employee assistance program personnel.

Order *Professional Counselor* today and take advantage of our special introductory offer: One year of *Professional Counselor* (6 bimonthy issues) for just $20.00. That's 23% off the regular subscription price!

Clip and mail to:

Professional Counselor, P.O. Box 607, Mount Morris, IL 61054-7641

YES! Enter my subscription to *Professional Counselor* for a full year (6 bimonthly issues) for only $20.00—23% off the regular subscription price. If you are not completely satisfied, simply return the subscription invoice marked CANCEL. The first issue will be yours to keep.

Name: _____

Address: _____

City: _____ State: _____ Zip: _____

❏ Payment enclosed   Charge my: ❏ Visa   ❏ MC

_____ Exp.: _____

Signature: _____

Please allow 4-6 weeks for delivery. FL residents please add $1.20 state sales tax.